D1369613

Molten rock pours into the sea, raising vast clouds
of acrid steam amid hissing, explosions and fireworks.

HAWAI'I
LAND of
VOLCANOES

Copyright © 1999
by Mutual Publishing

No part of this book may be reproduced
in any form or by any electronic or
mechanical means, including information
storage and retrieval devices or systems,
without prior written permission from the
publisher, except that brief passages may
be quoted for reviews.

All rights reserved
Library of Congress Catalog Card
Number: 97-71436

All photos by Douglas Peebles unless
otherwise noted.

First Printing, November 2000
1 2 3 4 5 6 7 8 9

Softcover
ISBN 1-56647-154-0

Casebound
ISBN 1-56647-192-3

Design by Jane Hopkins

Mutual Publishing
1215 Center Street, Suite 210
Honolulu, Hawaii 96816
Telephone (808) 732-1709
Fax (808) 734-4094
e-mail: mutual@lava.net
www.mutualpublishing.com

Printed in Taiwan

Multiple lava rivers flow from the growing
cone at Puʻu ʻŌʻō on the east rift zone of Kīlauea.

HAWAI'I
LAND of
VOLCANOES

Text by
JAN TᴇɴBRUGGENCATE

Photography by
DOUGLAS PEEBLES
G. BRAD LEWIS &
MICHAEL T. STEWART

MUTUAL PUBLISHING

Bright orange lava, having traveled miles from the vent atop Kīlauea's east rift zone, seeps from cracks in the face of a new basalt bench at the ocean's edge.

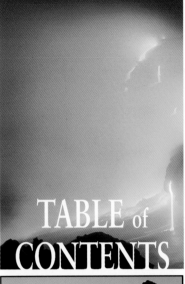

TABLE of CONTENTS

Top: A modern practitioner of ancient Hawaiian *hula* performs on the hard lava rock that formed the Hawaiian islands.

Center: The explosive zone where lava and sea meet creates stark landforms that quickly collapse or are overrun by further flows.

Bottom: The spores of the native 'ama'u fern quickly colonize young lava fields. Ferns are among the first kinds of plant life on new flows.

Molten lava explodes in a fiery display as it reaches the surface, then flows out over the still-cooling black rock that preceded it. G. Brad Lewis

Preface

Hawai'i's VOLCANOES ARE entirely appropriate to these islands. The climate here is balmy. The seas are warm and inviting. And the volcanoes are well-behaved, not explosive.

Most of the time.

Visitors by the busload drive around Kīlauea's summit crater and brave the fumes to peer into its heart, the fire pit Halema'uma'u. They walk trails where they can be warmed by vents of steam. And they see offerings left by people who pay respect to the old gods. A stone wrapped in a couple of leaves of the *kī* plant. A wreath of ferns. A cluster of dried *'ōhelo* berries thrown far from the bush from which they were picked, a traditional offering to the old goddess of fire, Pele. If you had been there when the offering was made, you'd hear, in Hawaiian or English, a quiet prayer:

"O Pele, here are some *'ōhelo* fruit for you. I also take some for myself."

Gods and Volcanoes

Long ago Hawai'i's chiefs pronounced the Polynesian gods defeated and replaced them with the Christian God, but many ancient traditions live on. And occasionally, the placid Hawaiian volcanoes remind residents of the tempers of the old gods. Sometimes earthquakes rip open great chasms in the ground where roads used to be. Eruptions build new mountains while lava flows destroy whole villages. But even these violent events leave just the tiniest impressions on the broader picture of Hawai'i's geology. The last few million years of the islands have seen a constant exchange between biology and geology. Vegetation takes hold almost as soon as the lava cools, although often another flow roars down to retake the same terrain. Scientists find charcoal between old lava flows, and the molds of trees surrounded and burned millennia ago. The history of these islands which goes back 75 million years or more spans most of the width of the Pacific Ocean. It is part of the story of how our planet works.

This volume, in words and pictures, provides a hint of the wonders of Hawai'i's volcanic world. A little geology, a little history, and always, the threat of destruction that attends every one of the world's active volcanoes.

Top: Native Hawaiians in traditional garb participate in the *Ka Ho'ola'a Ana* investiture ceremony at Kīlauea Caldera.

Center: A smoking lava flow enters the rural community of Kalapana, where every home would eventually be destroyed.

Bottom: Plants find places to take root in the smallest cracks in lava flows, as here at Hawai'i Volcanoes National Park.

Dancers bearing *hoʻokupu*, or gifts, at
Ka Hoʻolaʻa Ana investiture ceremony at Kīlauea Caldera.

Hawaiian Traditions, Creation Myths, Pele

THE EARLY HAWAIIANS had a range of tales about the origin of their Islands. *Kumulipo*, the great creation chant speaks, of heat in connection with the forming of the Earth. The growth of corals is also celebrated along with legendary stones that breed, producing more stones.

The Māui myth, which spread across Polynesia, has the demigod out fishing in his canoe when he hooked the bottom of the sea. With powerful jerks on the line he hauled up one island after another. But generally fire, not water, is at the center of myths about the creation of land.

Hawaiian Traditions

There are many Hawaiian traditions involving the volcanic origins of the Islands. A volcano was seen as being a living, feeling person or persons. Hawaiian historian Samuel Kamakau writes that when Kamehameha offered prayers and a sacrificial pig to the lava flows threatening his fishpond at Kīholo, "there were eyes in the lava to see Kamehameha, and ears to hear his appeals and his words of prayer, and the great blazing lava flow died down." Kamakau also speaks of the individual spirits, *ahi ʻai honua*, fires that eat the earth, which direct volcanic devastation from one place to another. But while there are many minor gods of the volcano, the greatest fire deity was, and still is, Pele.* She is said to act with complete independence but also through others, her sisters and relatives. These can take human forms, others remain spirits and can change from flesh and blood to being a spirit, and back again.

The Pele legends suggest that the goddess and her family arrived in Hawaiʻi after the Islands had been formed but were still erupting. William Westervelt, who collected and translated many Hawaiian myths, recounts that she got to the Island of Hawaiʻi only to find another volcano god already in place. His name was ʻAilaʻau, eater of the forest, and he lived at Kīlauea amidst its fiery lava fountains.

*Ancient practices of worship continue to be conducted by Native Hawaiians (particularly those who track their genealogy back to the goddess herself).

Top: Native Hawaiian practitioners offer traditional forms of respect at the edge of Halemaʻumaʻu.

Center: Performers wear head *lei* of plants gathered in the forests, and wrist pieces carefully crafted of native fibers.

Bottom: Headpieces in the ancient style are woven of the aerial roots of the ʻieʻie vine.

Māui's Islands

In Hawai'i, Māui uses his favorite fishhook, baited with an *'alae* or mudhen, to catch the sea floor and haul up the islands. In one version of the story, one of the *'alae*'s wings has been hidden, preventing Māui from completing the job, so instead of hauling up one large piece of land, he is left with a series of islands.

In other versions Māui is attempting to pull the separated islands together. His brothers, who are paddling his canoe, violate his order not to look back. When they do so, the fishing line breaks, and the Hawaiian islands drift back into their original places.

PAINTING BY RALPH KAGEHIRO

Legend says he saw Pele coming and instantly recognized her superior power. At that point, 'Aila'au disappeared without confronting her.

Pele's Voyage

Like all the early Hawaiians, the fire goddess voyaged to the Islands by canoe. Pele belonged to a family of demigods who controlled natural phenomena such as steam, rain, wind, thunder, lightning and explosions. In one legend, she arrived from the south in a canoe sailed by her brother, Kamohoali'i, and carrying her tiny sister, Hi'iaka. In some versions, she captained the canoe herself. Still other versions claimed that the lusty Pele was driven out of the family homeland because of an affair with a sister's husband. After journeying to various islands in the South Pacific, Pele arrived at the distant shores of Hawai'i.

The fire goddess immediately searched for a home by repeatedly digging in rock and looking for heat and lava. She started on Ni'ihau, moved to Kaua'i and on down the island chain. Various pits, caves and volcanic cones on each island were the results of Pele's efforts. Often, she struck water—her enemy—as at the Waikapala'e and Waikanaloa Wet Caves of Hā'ena, and Nomilu Pond on south Kaua'i. Her heat produced clouds of steam that made such places unsuitable, and she had to move on.

Paoa, The Digging Stick

Pele named her powerful digging stick Paoa. When she drove it into the mountains of Kaua'i, she created the steep slope still called Pu'ukapele. According to the story, the smoke of her activity was visible to her still-angry sister who had been cheated in love. She arrived to fight Pele, won the battle, and left the fire goddess for dead. Pele, however, survived and moved on in her quest for a home. She dug on O'ahu at Ke-'ālia-pa'a-kai (Salt Lake) and at Lē'ahi (Diamond Head). Neither location proved satisfactory. On the neighboring Island of Maui she again faced another battle with her sisters on the slopes of Haleakalā. Pele was again defeated, this time soundly, and the remains of her lava rock skeleton can still be seen, strewn across the Kahiki-nui coastline. The features are still known as Na-Iwi-O-Pele, the bones of Pele. But while her body had been defeated, Pele's spirit survived, and she finally traveled to Kīlauea on the Island of Hawai'i to make her home. Her angry sister, watching from afar, saw Pele's spirit moving in the clouds, and realized that Pele had ascended to a new plane. No mortal would never again be able to defeat the goddess of the volcano.

Top: The glow of the volcano's lava is reflected in clouds of smoke and steam rising over the vent.
MICHAEL T. STEWART

Center: Twisted sinews of rock are among the shapes of *pāhoehoe* flows. MICHAEL T. STEWART

Bottom: Incandescent streams of orange rock flow over the edge of a low rise and into the water below.
MICHAEL T. STEWART

The camera catches fragments of
glowing lava blasted through the
smoke of a coastal explosion.
MICHAEL T. STEWART

The ropelike texture of *pāhoehoe* lava oozes out over older flows.
Michael T. Stewart

Pele's Wrath

Local legends have Pele appearing frequently in human form, often testing the people she meets. Many of the lava flows sent from the volcano are viewed as expressions of her anger. According to one story, two girls were cooking breadfruit when Pele arrived in disguise. One girl was generous to the unknown visitor, but the other refused to give up her food. The first was warned and saved, but the home of the second girl was destroyed by a flow of lava.

The temperamental Pele also had legendary battles with the demigod Kamapua'a. He could change himself into a pig, a man or a variety of plants. Like Pele, Kamapua'a had a strong, influential family. When he courted her, and she rejected him, calling him "a pig and the son of a pig," they fought, each calling on powerful relatives for help.

Pele sent flames and lava flows. Kamapua'a responded with fogs and rainstorms. When she called her brothers to fight

Below: **A breeze off the land carries clouds of steam away from the black sand beach created by shattered bits of shiny lava.**

A dense smoke cloud envelopes the glowing interface between rock and sea.

Dripping lava, often flash-hardened by waves,
forms fascinating images along the shoreline.

Kamapua'a, his relatives made a beautiful woman appear and lured the brothers away. Then Kamapua'a sent a flood into Kīlauea to put out Pele's fires. Her brothers and uncles kept the fires alive, and attacked Kamapua'a once more. Ultimately, the two combatants became lovers, but the relationship remained volatile. They divided up the Island of Hawai'i, with Pele taking control of the hotter, drier districts of Puna, Ka'ū and Kona, where today lava flows are still common. Kamapua'a took the wet, green lands of Hilo, Hāmākua and Kohala. But their violent quarrels still occur when volcanic activity invades Kamapua'a's land, as when Mauna Loa flows reach into the Hilo district.

Sacrifices to Pele

Kamapua'a, in his pig form, was believed responsible for rooting up the ground, and was used by early Hawaiians to explain deep gullies and land, apparently torn up by supernatural forces. In the worship of Pele, any forms into which the male demigod was able to change himself, preferably a pig, are acceptable sacrifices. It was common when visiting the volcano to make offerings to Pele whenever one took something from an area controlled by her. For example, if 'o¯helo berries were collected, a few would be tossed into Kī¯lauea crater for the goddess. But one hearsay account illustrates a powerful break. In 1824, the chiefess Kapi'olani, who had been converted to Christianity, was said to have dealt a terminal blow to the common worship of Pele. She confronted the volcano goddess, read from the Bible, ate 'o¯helo berries without making offerings, and threw stones into Kī¯lauea crater. After she waited for Pele to respond, the volcano remained silent, and Kapi'olani was unhurt. Pele was declared defeated.

Top: The play of lava and rock, light and smoke, creates surreal landscapes on Kīlauea.

Center: White smoke, black rock, and a bit of orange show that this landscape is still changing in dramatic ways.

A lava lake bubbles and roils inside
an open-sided low cone atop Kīlauea's east rift zone.

Center of the Earth, Hot Spots and Plate Theory

WE TEND TO think of the atmosphere and oceans as fluids in constant motion, and of the Earth as solid. But study of the earth has shown the structure of our planet is anything but static. It is a constantly moving system. Rocks roll and land slides on the surface. Great plates that form the planet's crust shift, causing earthquakes and tsunami. The mantle of the Earth sags under the weight of the highest mountains, and recovers as those mountains erode away. Solid rock melts, its lighter elements rise and heavier ones sink. The fluid material of lava moves in currents deep under the Earth, and if it can find a way to the surface, the planet erupts.

Internal Heat

Some of the planet's incredibly intense heat is left over from its formation. Radioactive material in the heart of the planet also creates extremely hot temperatures. But much of Hawai'i's heat comes from mantle rock that has melted, forming magma, molten rock that is still underground. Once magma erupts to the surface, it is called lava. When lava hardens, or magma hardens underground, it is called igneous rock. Our planet has a solid inner core, believed to be made up of high percentages of iron and nickel. The inner core, about 1,500 miles in diameter, is surrounded by a fluid outer core. This is primarily iron and has more other elements than the inner core. The temperature of the molten outercore registers some 7,000 degrees Fahrenheit. The diameter of both the inner and outer cores is about 4,000 miles. In 1996 scientists discovered that together the cores spin independently of the mantle, generating a magnetic field. They appear to turn in the same direction as the rest of the Earth, but slightly faster, gaining a quarter turn every century. This discovery came about at Columbia University's Lamont-Doherty Earth Observatory when the seismic waves from natural earthquakes were studied. The combined core is hotter than the surface of the sun. And it is under incredible pressure from all the layers of material

Top: A skylight permits a view of an underground river of lava.

Center: Flowing lava breaks out across the Kamoamoa coastline.
MICHAEL T. STEWART

Bottom: Massive clouds of steam and smoke betray the region where lava enters the ocean.

SEISMIC TESTING

Science has few tools for testing the core of the planet. The work has been done primarily through seismic measurements, which study the reflections of energy waves traveling through the ground. Based on those and other measurements, scientists theorize that temperature doesn't increase uniformly with increased depth, and that pressures also vary somewhat. So molten areas tend to alternate with solid areas.

The top layer of the outer core is called the mantle, which geologists believe can be subdivided into several distinct portions. These are made up of a mixture of lighter elements than the core, and molten sections. Outside the mantle, the hard layer at the surface of the planet is called the crust. It is thinner under oceans, where it might be just 4 to 6 miles deep, and thicker under continents, where it may be 20 miles deep. The molten areas beneath the crust provide the magma that feeds volcanoes.

Cracks in the hardened surface of the lava lake at the Pu'u 'Ō'ō vent at Kīlauea reveal the molten lava below.

around it, which are pressing down under the influence of gravity. Molten rock heats up deep in the Earth, but its melting temperature changes with pressure. The higher the pressure, the more heat is required to change rock from its solid to liquid state. Although the outer core of the Earth already has a very high pressure, the 7,000-degree-plus temperature is so high that the surrounding rock has liquefied. Deeper down, the pressure increases so dramatically that even higher temperatures have no effect and the iron core is solid.

Tectonic Plate Theory

Most volcanoes are found in areas where the planet's tectonic plates meet. The Earth's surface is divided into these plates. They are often described as similar in appearance to the sections on the back of a turtle. Or imagine the pattern on a soccer ball.

Tectonic plate theory is fairly recent, having been developed in the 1960s. The Hawaiian Island chain played a major role in the formation of the theory. Geologists noted that Hawai'i is a long line of peaks, and originally they believed all the islands appeared at roughly the same time, arising from some kind of geologic rift. But more recent geological work that allowed the dating of the lava flows has indicated that the oldest islands are at the far northwest end of the chain, and the youngest are at the southeast, near the Island of Hawai'i. They also noticed the same pattern on two other island groups on the Pacific plate. All three chains, though hundreds or thousands of miles apart, form lines that run parallel to each other. The theory developed from this information was that each chain was developing over a "hot spot," where magma melts through the crust to create volcanoes. The theory further concluded that the entire floor of the Pacific Ocean was moving westward at a steady rate. As the Pacific plate moved, the hot spot remained relatively fixed. The line of volcanoes left behind gives an indication of the direction of the plane's movement.

Major Tectonic Plates

The Pacific Plate is just one of several that cover the Earth's surface. Some geologists count seven large plates and two dozen or more smaller ones. Among the major ones is the North American Plate, which includes all of North America and about half of the North Atlantic Ocean. The South American Plate has most of South America and

Top: Mauna Kea and Mauna Loa are visible in the distance, breaking through the volcanic smog and clouds. Kohala can be seen in the foreground.

Center: New lava beaches and bays are formed as lava continually rolls into the sea.

Bottom: Volcanic landforms, near and far. G. Brad Lewis

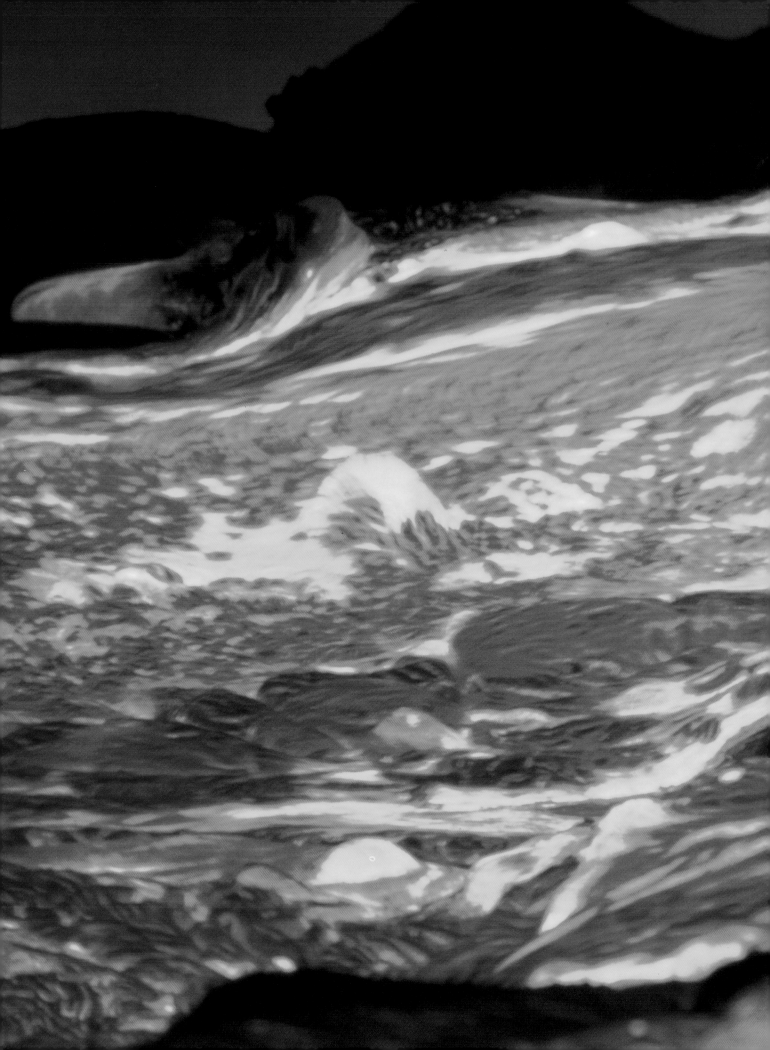

A wide river of *pāhoehoe* lava runs
through Hawai'i Volcanoes
National Park.
G. BRAD LEWIS

approximately half the South Atlantic. A single plate accounts for most of Asia and Europe, there is one for Africa, and one that forms Antarctica. Australia lies on the last major plate, which includes parts of the Indian Ocean and the western South Pacific. The small Nazca Plate is under the eastern South Pacific, between the Pacific and South American plates, and bounded on the south by the Antarctica Plate.

Ring of Fire

All the tectonic plates are separated by cracks in the planet's crust, and they move toward or away from each other. The points where the plates meet are some of the most geologically active places on Earth. The circumference of the Pacific Plate is sometimes called the Ring of Fire, for the number of active volcanoes that exist along the boundary. Tectonic plates slide laterally in some areas, as at the San Andreas Fault in California. In other areas they spread apart, with the intervening space filled with magma rising from the Earth's mantle. There are also subduction zones where two plates are pushed into each other, one sliding up over another while the lower plate is driven back into the mantle. And there are active volcanoes like those found at the Hawaiian hot spot.

Opposite page: Fast-moving volcanic rivers find easy routes around obstructions on their way from the mountain to the sea.

Left: One of the steep-sided spatter cones formed by Kīlauea's long-running eruption leaves dramatic evidence of its power. G. Brad Lewis

This spectacular rainforest, a complex ecosystem of canopy trees, tall ferns and smaller trees, and ground-level mosses and shrubs, fills the aging lava flows with life.

THE
HAWAIIAN ARCHIPELAGO

THREE

A HOT SPOT is an area where superheated rock moves from deep within the Earth's mantle upward toward the center crust. And while the Pacific Plate moves, the Hawaiian Hot Spot remains fixed in relation to the planet as a whole. Some scientists believe the plate "floats" on a bed of magma that is forced up from deeper in the Earth, and is pushed out laterally in all directions beneath the crust. The Pacific Plate is believed to be moving slowly but steadily at the rate of about three inches a year. When a thermal plume forms a hot spot, magma pushes through the crust to erupt. Initially, as with the Hawaiian hot spot, much of that magma erupted under water millions of years ago. Yet that same process is going on now with the undersea volcano, Lōʻihi, about 20 miles off the east coast of the Island of Hawaiʻi. Geologists theorize that the upwelling of magma finds its way to the surface through cracks that become permanent supply routes, feeding underground magma storage chambers beneath the summits of various volcanoes. There is a huge amount of magma available, and it is capable of supporting several active eruptions. Lōʻihi, Kīlauea and Mauna Loa are all being fed by the same Hawaiian hot spot. Sometimes, two of these erupt simultaneously.

Dating the Hot Spot

Geologists have determined that the Hawaiian Hot Spot has been in place and building volcanoes on the Pacific Plate for 75 to 80 million years. They have calculated this by analyzing the rocks in various volcanic features, including the most ancient, like Meiji Seamount, which has been dated at around 75 million years old. Some believe that our island chain may be much older, but that the evidence has disappeared with the collision of the Pacific Plate and the plates to the north and west. The line of the Hawaiian chain moves roughly northwest from Hawaiʻi to the Seamount of Daikakuji, where it changes to the Emperor Seamounts. Seamounts are mountains whose

Top: Surf rolls incessantly onto the coastline, promoting the erosion of the islands' rocky fringes.

Center: The peaks of twin Hawaiian shield volcanoes catch the sunlight above the clouds.

Bottom: ʻAkaka Falls on the Hāmākua coast of Hawaiʻi plunges over a basalt precipice, through dense vegetation.

THE HAWAIIAN HOT SPOT & THE PACIFIC PLATE

Many scientists believe magma is moving toward the surface in a steady stream, but that it erupts only intermittently.

If you repeatedly tap a pencil tip on a moving piece of paper, you get a line of dots. That's the process with the Hawaiian hot spot and the Pacific Plate. The ocean floor which forms most of the Pacific plate is like the moving piece of paper, and the hot spot is the pencil, repeatedly dotting it with islands.

There are roughly 125 volcanoes between the current hot spot and where the Hawaiian/ Emperor chain disappears at its unknown point of origin.

One of the vents during Kīlauea's long-running eruption.
G. BRAD LEWIS

peaks are below the surface of the ocean. Some of them may once have been islands, but due to erosion and subsidence their summits are now below sea level. A few are believed to have spent millions of years as atolls before subsiding. Once sunken, these former atolls are called guyots.

Meiji's Voyage

The same hot spot that is today producing Lōʻihi also produced Meiji, 3,700 miles away. Because the Pacific Plate is in constant motion, after the hot spot forms a volcano, the plate's movement pulls the volcano and the seafloor around it away from the hot spot.

From the time of Meiji's creation to about 43 million years ago—about the time the Seamount of Daikakuji was formed— the Pacific plate moved in a northward direction. Then, the direction changed and the chain began moving in a more westerly direction. Today the island farthest from the hot spot is Kure Atoll, whose volcanic parts have sunk below the surface, but whose coral reefs are constantly growing and keeping up with its slow subsidence. Closer to the hot spot one finds Midway Atoll, Pearl and Hermes Reef, Lisianski and Laysan islands, and Maro Reef. These have only the products of the living coral reef at the surface.

Volcanic Islands

Roughly half the distance from Kure to the current hot spot is the first surface evidence of the chain's volcanic origins. The basalt, or volcanic rock, remnants called Gardner Pinnacles pierce the ocean's surface. Nearer the main Hawaiian Islands are the French Frigate Shoals, entirely made up of reefs and sand bars, and accompanied by a fragment of the volcanic island that forms their base: La Perouse Pinnacle, a chunk of rock white with the guano of the seabirds that roost there.

Nearer still are Necker and Nihoa, the islands closest to the main Hawaiian chain that hint at human habitation. The only remaining evidence consists of a few shelters and rock altars left behind. Finally, 300 miles and five or six million years away from the original hot spot are the oldest of the major islands, Kauaʻi and Niʻihau. Oʻahu's most ancient rock has an age of only three million years, and Maui is a relative youngster, just a million years old.

The islands of Maui County—Maui, Molokaʻi, Lanaʻi and Kahoʻolawe—although created by several separate volcanoes, are believed to have once been a single island now called Maui Nui. Subsidence of the volcanoes, rising

Top: Haleakalā is a large volcanic mountain, over 10,000 feet above sea level, that forms the eastern part of the Island of Maui.

Center: Wailua Falls and Wailua River drain a vast central region of the island of Kauaʻi, including rain from Mt. Waiʻaleʻale, one of the wettest spots on Earth.

Bottom: Kauaʻi's Nā Pali coast and the rugged northwest-facing cliffs are the result of five million years of erosion by wind, rain and sea.

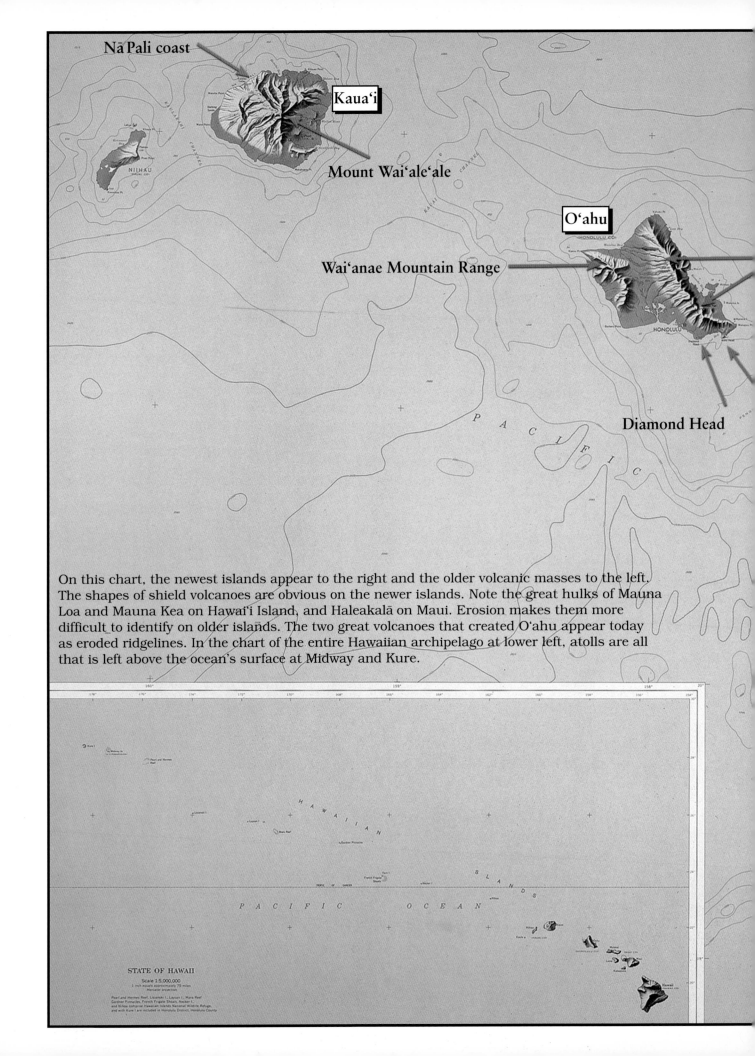

Nā Pali coast

Kaua'i

Mount Wai'ale'ale

O'ahu

Wai'anae Mountain Range

Diamond Head

On this chart, the newest islands appear to the right and the older volcanic masses to the left. The shapes of shield volcanoes are obvious on the newer islands. Note the great hulks of Mauna Loa and Mauna Kea on Hawai'i Island, and Haleakalā on Maui. Erosion makes them more difficult to identify on older islands. The two great volcanoes that created O'ahu appear today as eroded ridgelines. In the chart of the entire Hawaiian archipelago at lower left, atolls are all that is left above the ocean's surface at Midway and Kure.

STATE OF HAWAII
Scale 1:5,000,000

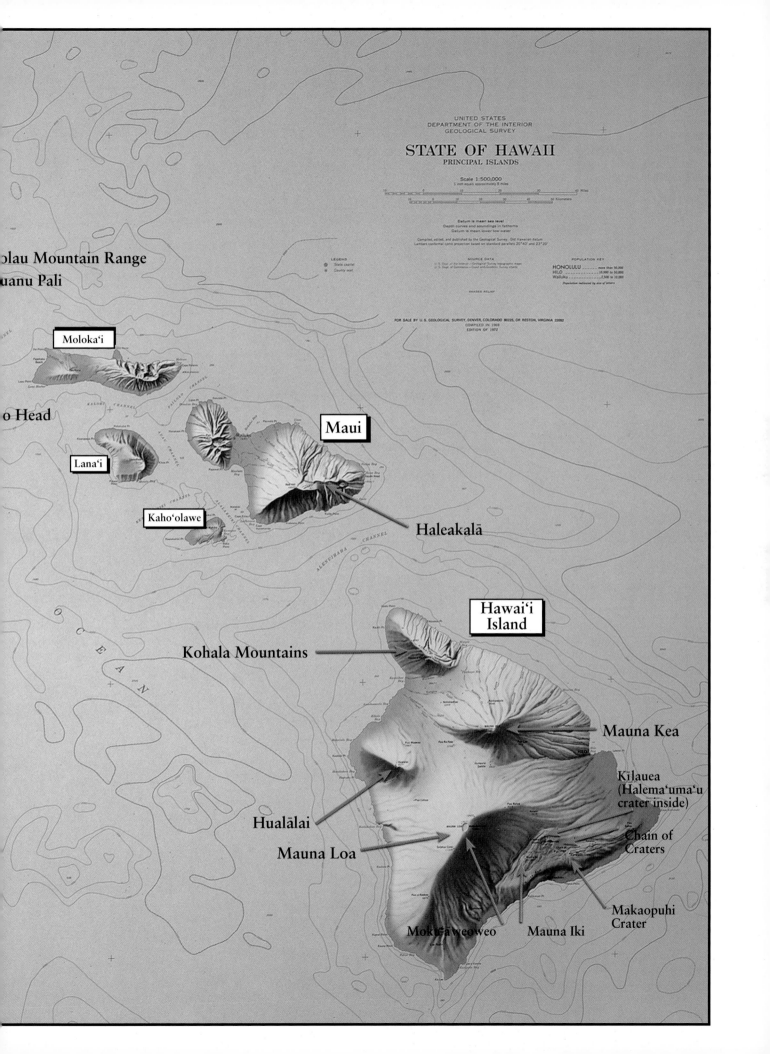

UNITED STATES
DEPARTMENT OF THE INTERIOR
GEOLOGICAL SURVEY

STATE OF HAWAII
PRINCIPAL ISLANDS

Scale 1:500,000
1 inch equals approximately 8 miles

Datum is mean sea level
Depth curves and soundings in fathoms
Datum is mean, lower low water

Compiled, edited, and published by the Geological Survey. Old Hawaiian datum
Lambert conformal conic projection based on standard parallels 20°40' and 23°20'

SOURCE DATA
U.S. Dept. of the Interior—Geological Survey topographic maps
U.S. Dept. of Commerce—Coast and Geodetic Survey charts

LEGEND
State capital
County seat

POPULATION KEY
HONOLULU .... more than 50,000
HILO .... 10,000 to 50,000
Wailuku .... 2,500 to 10,000

Population indicated by size of letters

SHADED RELIEF

FOR SALE BY U.S. GEOLOGICAL SURVEY, DENVER, COLORADO 80225, OR RESTON, VIRGINIA 22092
COMPILED IN 1969
EDITION OF 1972

olau Mountain Range

uanu Pali

Moloka'i

o Head

Lana'i

Kaho'olawe

Maui

Haleakalā

Hawai'i Island

Kohala Mountains

Mauna Kea

Kīlauea
(Halema'uma'u
crater inside)

Hualālai

Mauna Loa

Chain of
Craters

Makaopuhi
Crater

Mokuʻāweoweo   Mauna Iki

Cinder cones lead to the snowy summit of Mauna Kea, where astronomical observatories keep watch.

sea levels and erosion have created comparatively shallow ocean channels where at one time there were valleys between the peaks of Maui Nui. In such a natural manner that spans many millennia, groups of islands are created.

On the Island of Hawai'i however, five distinct volcanoes are still connected above the sea's surface: Kohala, Mauna Kea, Hualālai, Mauna Loa and Kīlauea. This volatile area still has a great deal to show for itself, and its story is far from over.

Left: The abrupt sinking of shorelines during big earthquakes forces coastal vegetation into the tidal zone where salt water kills it.

Below: A lava bubble explodes near the ocean, tossing up streamers of molten rock that are deadly despite its fluid, graceful appearance. G. BRAD LEWIS

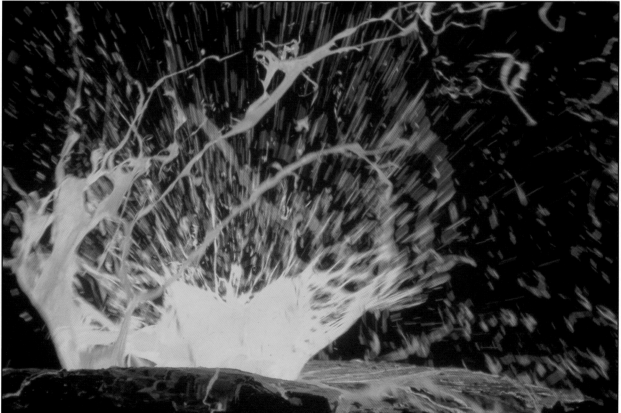

Molokini, an open-sided tuff cone off Maui,
is a favorite dive tour destination.

Individual
Islands

ONCE MAGMA CRACKS through the crust at a new location over the hot spot and starts building an island, it begins a process of volcanic activity that may last millions of years. The initial eruptions release comparatively small amounts of lava, then in the shield-building stage most of a volcano's volume is deposited. Finally, the activity slows down. Eruptions which occur later may be hundreds or thousands of years apart. Haleakalā is close to a million years old and looks like an extinct volcano, but erupted as recently as about 200 years ago.

The initial structure of an Hawaiian volcano is believed to be a cone with steep sides. Lōʻihi, the undersea volcano off the southeast coast of the Island of Hawaiʻi has this shape and is an example of the early stage of activity, which geologists call the preshield phase.

Rift Zones

A volcano begins developing rift zones early in its life. These are interior areas of weakness generally leading outward from the summit, and are the site of many and varied eruptions. Rift zones develop into major sources of lavas that broaden the growing volcanic structure. Lōʻihi already has two rift zones, one extending to the south of its summit and a smaller one to the north.

When a new volcano's pre-shield phase is over—after a few hundred thousand years—its eruptions increase in frequency and produce more and more lava. The flows spread out, pile on top of each other, and the shape of the volcano changes from a steep-sided cone to a shield, whose sides run out at a shallow angle. Most of the Hawaiian islands are believed to have been in the shield-building phase when they reached the ocean's surface, a period geologists feel was associated with a great deal of explosive activity as the ocean and magma met. Kīlauea, the most active of the Hawaiian volcanoes, is in its shield-building period. It has extensive rift zones to the east and southwest.

Top: Haleakalā rises to more than 10,000 feet and has a pitted, rugged landscape unlike the rainforests at lower elevations.

Center: Knife-edge ridges of Kauaʻi's Nā Pali are typical of an old, long-dormant volcanic region—now lush, green, and deeply eroded.

Bottom: Protected Hanauma Bay, Oʻahu's premier location for safe, nearshore snorkeling, clearly shows its origin as a volcano crater.

Lāna'i island, once a part of the
giant island of Maui Nui, now
stands alone across the channel from
Maui, Moloka'i and Kaho'olawe.

Rugged cliffs on the north coast of Moloka'i were formed by
an immense landslide which may have instantly obliterated
nearly half the island.

By the time a major Hawaiian volcano nears the end of its shield-building phase, its peak can be thousands of feet above sea level, and the frequency of its eruptions tapers off. Mauna Loa, which still erupts on average every 10 years or so, is believed to be near the end of its shield-building phase.

Erosion and Subsidence

Hawaiian volcanoes may be nearing a million years in age when most eruptive activity stops. By this time, the moving Pacific Plate has pulled the volcano 30 or 40 miles away from where the hot spot first began feeding it, and it no longer has a short, direct source to the magma under the Earth's mantle. Now erosion and subsidence become the major factors in geologic change. On the Island of Hawai'i, Hualālai volcano is past its major shield-building phase; it erupts every few hundred years. Mauna Kea is considered dormant, since it hasn't erupted for more than 4,000 years, and there is no indication it will erupt again any time soon. Kohala Mountains represent the remainder of a volcano which last erupted perhaps 60,000 years ago during a post-shield building session. Māhukona was the first Hawai'i island volcano, but never reached the height of others. Most of it is now underwater or buried under the lavas of Kohala and Hualālai eruptions.

Hawai'i is still evolving and illustrates both ends of the volcano spectrum. While Māhukona is gone, and Lō'ihi is still underwater and growing. Scientists at the Volcano Observatory figure that Lō'ihi will eventually develop a surface connection with Hawai'i island. In several hundred thousand years, the Kohala Mountains are expected to have subsided sufficiently to form a separate island.

Maui Nui

Some separation of land has already occurred in what is now Maui County which includes four islands. At its largest the land mass called Maui Nui was one and a half times larger than Hawai'i island is today. Years ago, it encompassed the volcanoes that presently form West Maui, East Maui, Kaho'olawe, East Moloka'i, West Moloka'i, Lāna'i, and the shallow waters between Moloka'i and O'ahu called Penguin Bank. Over eons, because of island subsidence and the effects of various ice ages, parts of Maui Nui were either exposed or submerged, creating the separate islands as they are today.

Once the shield-building phase of activity is over, some volcanoes stop erupting altogether. Others enter a post-shield phase, during which they can pour out thick

Top: The view from Kalalau Lookout on Kaua'i shows the dramatically eroded landscape of Nā Pali from an elevation of 4,000 feet.

Center: The sun, hidden behind the clouds off Kāneohe Bay on O'ahu, spreads rays of light over the ocean.

Bottom: Beaches like this one near Princeville on Kaua'i are built on reefs, and are made up primarily of bits of coral and pieces of shell.

DIAMOND HEAD

The famous Diamond Head, known in early Hawai'i as Lē'ahi, is an example of several huge tuff cones on O'ahu such as Pūowaina (Punchbowl) and Koko Head. These are accumulated cinders and ash and are part of the rejuvenation phase of Hawaiian volcanoes. In many cases, a million years or more after the shield-building phase of an island's development has ended, smaller eruptions break through to the surface, creating cones like these, and lava flows much younger than those that originally formed the island.

Several of the smaller islands of the Hawaiian chain, including Ka'ula near Ni'ihau, and Molokini near Maui, are tuff cones from a rejuvenation phase.

Pūowaina (Punchbowl), on the Island of Oʻahu, is another example of Hawaiʻi's many tuff cones. This view of the edge shows the originally porous rock packed into a more solid mass by the passing of time. Little remains to suggest that this rock was once layers of cinders and ash.

flows of lava that obscure many of their distinctive summit features from the shield-building phase. Kaua'i, for example, has canyons thousands of feet deep that some geologists feel were formed by a separate volcano and suggests millions of years of erosion. But the island also has comparatively uneroded volcanic cones, and even spatter cones with fresh-looking cinder. Lavas in the Po'ipū area, on the dry leeward side of Kaua'i, still have the appearance of fresh flows. Modern techniques for dating volcanic rocks imply that while the majority of the rocks on Kaua'i are in the range of five million years old, other cones scattered around the island erupted only a half million to 1.5 million years ago. This apparent contradiction is termed rejuvenation. However, it isn't particularly common. Rejuvenated phase features are not found on O'ahu's Wai'anae coast range, or in the West Moloka'i mountains. West Maui has only a few rejuvenation features, around the Lahaina area.

However, researchers say East Maui's Haleakalā, still in its rejuvenated stage, is a potentially dangerous volcano. It probably erupts every few hundred years, and it's been more than 200 years since the last one. Nobody is guessing when the next Haleakalā eruption will occur. Maybe in a few years, perhaps in the next century, or the one after that.

Opposite page: Kaua'i's eroded cliffs are blanketed in green foliage except in the steepest, most eroded areas.

Below: The Ko'olau Gap at Haleakalā.

A slowly cooling river of lava
lies among slabs of *pāhoehoe*.

Early Writers View the Volcanoes

HAWAI'i's ACTIVE VOLCANOES overwhelmed early travelers. Most of them came in the era before photographs and videotape, and had never before seen anything like a live eruption.

Hiram Bingham

Evidently one visit made such an impression on the missionary Hiram Bingham that this devout man gave some leeway to a pagan goddess. He wrote of approaching Kīlauea in 1830: "Evidences of existing volcanic agency multiplied around us; steam, gas and smoke, issued from sulfur banks on the north-east and south-east sides of the crater, and here and there from deep and extended fissures connected with the fiery subterranean agency; and as we passed circumspectly along the apparently depressed plain that surrounds the crater, we observed an immense volume of smoke and vapor ascending from the midst of it. At the same time, and from the same source, various unusual sounds not easily described or explained, fell with increasing intensity on the ear. Then the angry abyss, the fabled habitation and throne of Pele, the great ex-goddess of the Hawaiians, opened before us."

Fathomless Molten Abyss

Bingham crawled on his knees to the edge of Kīlauea's crater, and described "a lake of lava, some black and indurated, some fiery and flowing, some cooling as a floating bridge over the fathomless molten abyss seven times hotter than Nebuchadnezzar's hottest furnace, and some bursting up through this temporary incrustation, rending it here and there, and forming mounts and cones upon it."

While the missionary made the point that Pele had been overthrown, the scene caused him to refer to the volcano deity as if she existed: "Had Vulcan employed ten thousand giant Cyclops, each with a steam engine of one-thousand horse-power, blowing anthracite coal for smelting mountain minerals, or heaving up and hammering to pieces rocks and

Top: A 19th Century artist's view of an active Hawaiian volcano.

Center: Viewing the lava lake at Kīlauea while standing on a cooled *pāhoehoe* flow.

Bottom: Many visitors were and still are stunned by the combination of stark, rocky terrain with the dense rainforest vegetation of Hawai'i's volcano country.

VOLCANO HOUSE

The summit of Kīlauea, with an elevation near 4,000 feet in rainforest country, has never been a place for comfortable overnight exposure to the elements. In the 1800s, it could take visitors on horseback or in carriages all day, or a couple of days, to get from the port at Hilo to the top. Since 1846 visitors have been able to spend the night at Volcano House.

It started as a grass shack pitched at the rim of the crater. The sugar grower who built it charged a dollar a night.

A larger, but still grass-thatched structure went up in 1866, and it was where every notable visitor to the volcano stayed, from the kings and queens of Hawai'i to traveling dignitaries like the writer Mark Twain. Apparently, it was an impressive improvement. Twain wrote in June of 1866: "The surprise of finding a good hotel in such an outlandish spot startled me considerably more than the volcano did. The house is new—built three or four months ago—and the table is good. There has never heretofore been anything in this locality for the accommodation of travellers but a crazy native grass hut."

That thatched Volcano House was replaced in 1877 by a more modern structure, whose beams were still made of trees cut in the forest. The new house, with fireplace and proper, swinging doors, still stands. It was moved from the crater's edge, and now houses the Volcano Art Center, where it supports the local arts community and also serves as a museum of the early days on the volcano.

The name most commonly associated with the operation of the hotel at the crater is George Lycurgus, who took over in the 1890s. The hotel he built and ran for decades burned in 1940 and was replaced a year later with the structure that still stands today, providing a crater rim view to visitors coming for a meal or a night's stay.

LYMAN HOUSE MEMORIAL MUSEUM

1926 FLOW
BEGAN 10 MILES ABOVE ROAD:
EXTENDS 4 MILES BELOW ROAD
TO OCEAN, WHERE IT DESTROYED
HOOPULOA VILLAGE APR 18 1926

Above: A quiet sitting area in the Volcano House once run by "Uncle" George Lycurgus. For Hawai'i it had the rare furnishing touch of a fireplace for warmth on cool Kīlauea nights. BAKER-VAN DYKE COLLECTION

Left: Early visitors inspect a lava flow which wiped out the coastal village of Ho'ōpūloa. BAKER-VAN DYKE COLLECTION

hills, their united efforts would but begin to compare with the work of Pele here." Later, while traveling across the lava flows of the Kona side, he reported: "At almost every step for sixty miles we were reminded of Pele's power. Our road was not Macadamized [meaning paved], but Peleized, and by no means inviting."

Mark Twain

The newspaper writer and humorist Mark Twain was in Hawai'i and visited Kīlauea in 1866. He downplayed the scene, saying he'd been disappointed: "The little fountains scattered about looked very beautiful. They boiled, and coughed, and spluttered, and discharged sprays of stringy red fire of about the consistency of mush, for instance from ten to fifteen feet into the air, along with a shower of brilliant white sparks a quaint and unnatural mingling of gouts of blood and snowflakes!" Twain added, with his characteristic wry humor: "The smell of sulfur is strong, but not unpleasant to a sinner."

Isabella Bird

A decade later, Isabella Bird wrote of her six-month visit to the Islands, including two visits to Kīlauea. She approached by horseback on a dark, rainy night, and wrote about the glow of the erupting volcano: "Is that possibly a pool of blood? I thought in horror, as a rain puddle glowed crimson on the track. Not that indeed! A glare brighter and redder than that from any furnace suddenly lightened the whole sky, and from that moment brightened our path."

The next day, Bird and her party climbed down into the crater and walked over a recent lava flow: "It was so hot that a shower of rain hissed as it fell upon it. The crust became increasingly insecure and necessitated our walking in single file, with the guide in front, to test the security of the footing. I fell through several times, and always into holes full of sulfurous steam, so malignantly acid that my dog-skin gloves were burned through as I raised myself on my hands."

When they reached the edge of the fire pit, Halema'uma'u, she wrote: "I think we all screamed, I know we all wept, but we were all speechless, for a new glory and terror had been added to the earth. It is the most unutterable of wonderful things. The words of common speech are quite useless."

On a second trip to Kīlauea, she described the view of the lava lake: "The whole of the inside was red and molten, full of knobs, and great fiery stalactites. Jets of lava at a white heat wave thrown up constantly, and frequently the

Top: **Grass-thatched Volcano House, built in 1866, was a proper hotel, according to Mark Twain, who visited that year.** LYMAN HOUSE MEMORIAL MUSEUM

Center: **Volcano country is a maze of lava tubes and cracks, caverns and outcroppings, pits and craters. Here, in 1890, Ernest Lyman displays Kaūmana Cave above Hilo.** LYMAN HOUSE MEMORIAL MUSEUM

Bottom: **Peering over the crater's edge at Kīlauea is a dizzying experience, whether today or a century ago, although frequently there are safety railings built by the National Park Service.** LYMAN HOUSE MEMORIAL MUSEUM

Right, top: Throughout the latterpart of the 19th century, trips to Kīlauea's summit were horse-and-buggy affairs through dense native forest.

Right, bottom: This car was possibly abandoned in the path of aʻā lava advancing across Hoʻōpūloa Road on April 19, 1926.

Below: Early viewers are transfixed by the sight of lava entering the sea at Hoʻōpūloa in 1926. LYMAN HOUSE MEMORIAL MUSEUM

rent in the side spat our lava in clots, which cooled rapidly, and looked like drops of bottlegreen glass...The blast or roar which came up from below was more than deafening; it was stunning: and accompanied with heavy subterranean rumbling and detonations."

Anne Brassey

A few years later, Anne Brassey, in her 1881 volume, *A Voyage in the Sunbeam*, described Kīlauea during her visit on Christmas Eve, 1876: "We were standing on the extreme edge of a precipice, overhanging a lake of molten fire, a hundred feet below us, and nearly a mile across. Dashing against the cliffs on the opposite side, with a noise like the roar of a stormy ocean, waves of blood-red, fiery, liquid lava hurled their billows upon an iron-bound headland, and then rushed up the face of the cliffs to toss their gory spray in the air."

GREAT ACTIVE VOLCANO
KILAUEA NATIONAL PARK, HAWAII

Above: For travelers, the chance to see a live volcano was an irresistible combination of risky adventure that could be justified as educational. Best of all, it offered chills and thrills in the name of science. No where else on Earth could such huge lakes of lava be seen or rivers of molten rock, as depicted here— all of which was sure to inspire envy in those who stayed home.

POSTCARDS

Some visitors to Hawai'i took in the remarkable natural wonders of the islands, but instead of sending pictures of volcanoes, they mailed off images of where they stayed.

The top two were forms of advertising included without charge among the writing materials in a hotel room's desk drawer.

Today, these old images provide a view of period furnishings and architecture; the casual elegance of the Volcano House sunroom, with its wicker seating, flowers and palms, and windows framed in bright fabric. The exterior shot of the hotel shows an American flag, perhaps to remind folks that while Hawai'i in those days was far away, it was still an American territory.

Other cards used photography or dramatic artwork that provided details a photographer might have trouble obtaining. Note the careful placement of moon, molten spatter and flames in the card at lower right. Early card-makers sometimes added color to black-and-white photography, creating scenes that look unreal to today's eyes, but are actually pretty faithful to the original image.

In the days before instant photoprocessing, a card depicting other tourists amusing themselves was perhaps the best way to easily and quickly convey what you'd seen to the folks back home.

SUN PARLOR, VOLCANO HOUSE, HAWAII

PORTION OF HOTEL FRONTAGE, VOLCANO HOUSE, DIRECTLY OVERLOOKING CRATER, HAWAII.

VOLCANO OF KILAUEA · HAWAIIAN ISLANDS.

Published by the ISLAND CURIO CO. JAMES STEINER, Honolulu, Hawaiian Islands.   GERMANY.

KILAUEA VOLCANO HAWAII

Visitors in the Victorian era were often very determined, and they had to be at a time when comfort was usually unavailable. What mattered most to those willing to make a long sea voyage, and further trek inland, was the unparalleled opportunity to experience raw nature. America and Europe could not compete with the particularly amazing sights found on the Island of Hawai'i.

Tourism used to involve small groups—dozens, not thousands—and was likely a once-in-a-lifetime trip. The expense of travel in the 19th century often limited it to the wealthy. But adults of all kinds evidently couldn't resist the odd pleasure of posing together in warm caves, or scorching postcards for the sake of thrilling the recipients.

96 GREAT LAVA FISSURE, VOLCANO OF KILAUEA, HAWAIIAN ISLANDS.

241 TOURISTS EXPLORING HOT LAVA CAVES, VOLCANO KILAUEA, HAWAIIAN ISLANDS.

209 TOURISTS SCORCHING POST CARDS, VOLCANO OF KILAUEA, HAWAIIAN ISLANDS.

An automobile trapped by the lava flows near
Wahaʻula in Hawaiʻi Volcanoes National Park. MICHAEL T.
STEWART

Destruction
and Science

Hawai'i's VOLCANOES ARE known for their placid natures, as volcanoes go. They seldom explode or send hot ash-flows down mountainsides. Kīlauea is sometimes called the world's only "drive-in" volcano. Good roads lead to the very edge and down inside its caldera, the broad basin formed by the collapse of the volcano's cone. Trails twist among its steaming vents.

Levels of Destruction

Today, Hawai'i Volcanoes National Park invites people into the very heart of volcano country, so frighteningly described by Bingham, Twain, Bird and Brassey. Kīlauea's eruptions tend to be spectacular but not explosive, and despite the powerful language used by the early writers, such graphic descriptions were only possible because they could get close enough to the fire pit to see the flames, feel the rumbles and experience the heat. Kīlauea is the only readily-accessible erupting volcano that people flock to, instead of run from. When Mount St. Helens erupted in 1980, the devastation was immense. Pinatubo, in 1991 in the Philippines, destroyed villages and blanketed the entire planet with a thin cloud of volcanic particles. For several years, this ash in the atmosphere gave us spectacularly colorful sunsets. Before these incidents, the most spectacular world event was in Krakatoa which exploded in 1883, destroyed a whole island, and unleashed huge tsunami.

When most volcanoes in populated areas show signs of an impending eruption, emergency officials plan mass evacuations. Hawai'i County Civil Defense includes crowd control as one of its main tasks. However, Hawai'i residents and even mainlanders drop what they're doing and reserve seats on aircraft headed for the Island of Hawai'i. But volcanoes by their very nature destroy as well as create. While producing new land, they cover up the old and sear it with fire.

Top: Volcano scientists wearing protective gear collect samples of fresh rock. J.D. GRIGGS

Center: A family's home burns at Kalapana as lava pours through the yard in 1984.

Bottom: At the Jaggar Museum adjacent to the Hawaiian Volcano Observatory, seismagraphs record earth movements.

PELE FUMES

Early Polynesian residents of these islands feared Pele for good reason. She poured molten rock over their farms, villages, and fishponds.

On the other hand, Kamehameha had reason to feel he had a special relationship with the goddess. At his request, she halted the lava flow that would have destroyed his fishpond at Kīholo. And when the army of his rival, the chief Keoua, was crossing from Hilo to Ka'ū in 1790, many of the men died in a volcanic explosion. They were passing through the dry area south of Kīlauea caldera when the summit exploded, engulfing them in a cloud of acrid gas and ash. Many suffocated in the dense fumes. Warriors who followed them were amazed that so many of the dead had no visible injuries.

Center, top: **Fireworks near Kīlauea's Pu'u 'Ō'ō vent.**
G. Brad Lewis

Mauna Loa in its 1868 eruption caused a mudslide that destroyed a village; a 1926 flow overran the settlement of Hoʻōpūloa; in 1950 three separate flows to the ocean wiped out the village of Hoʻokena Mauka.

These infrequent eruptions can generate as much lava in a few days as Kīlauea does in weeks or months. Much of this hot rock stays high on the 13,700-foot mountain, but in some cases a flow will develop a distinct channel that directs it toward coastal settlements.

Preventing Destruction

Geologists have considered several methods to prevent destruction from lava flows. They've tried building high walls and spraying the molten rock with water. Aircraft were used experimentally to bomb Mauna Loa flows in 1935 and 1942. So far, no particular measure has been entirely effective.

One major problem: if you redirect lava, how do you decide whose property gets saved and whose is lost? This question has prevented heroic measures to redirect lava in more recent times. However, the Mauna Loa Observatory that stands at 11,000 feet has a huge protective dike of lava rock between it and the summit in an attempt to protect the buildings from being overrun by a fast-moving Mauna Loa flow.

The need to be able to understand and predict the behavior of the Hawaiʻi volcanoes, along with simple scientific curiosity, led to the study of volcanoes. This in turn led to the founding of a world-famous institution: the Hawaiian Volcano Observatory.

The Professional Study of Hawaiian Volcanoes

A number of factors recommended Hawaiʻi for specific research. Its volcanoes are eminently accessible. They are frequently active. And they are not so explosive that studying them puts scientists in physical danger. Many professional and lay volcanologists visited and studied the Hawaiian mountains throughout the 1800s, and detailed surveys were performed as early as the 1870s under the Hawaiian monarchy. But it wasn't until 1911 that the first permanent observatory was built. In that year, Massachusetts Institute of Technology scientist Thomas Jaggar and volcanologist Frank Perret established themselves at the rim of Halemaʻumaʻu. The Hawaiian Volcano Observatory was founded the next year with funding from both MIT and Hawaiʻi business officials. The work often involved active

Top: A Kalapana resident's two-story house catches fire, ignited by hot lava.

Center, bottom: A curious visitor stands at the edge of Kīlauea crater to get a closer look. G. Brad Lewis

Bottom: Video cameras capture the movement of fresh lava flows at Kīlauea. G. Brad Lewis

Opposite page: Homes blaze as lava pushes through the community of Kalapana.

Asphalt raises dark smoke as it burns under the steady advance of the flow.

A volcano scientist stands atop the rock crust that covers an active lava river, which can be seen through a skylight.

inventing, since equipment and techniques were required that no one had ever before envisioned.

Jaggar recognized the uniqueness of Hawai'i's volcano country, and joined in an effort to get the area named a national park. Kīlauea and the summit of Mauna Loa were included in a park established in 1916. The first observations of the volcano had been purely visual. But the arrival of scientists pushed the development of new measuring devices. Early thermometers were simply mixtures of materials that melted at different temperatures, which were inserted into the lava to get a rough idea of the heat of the molten rock.

With time and improved technology, the equipment got more sophisticated. By the 1940s, scientists still led by Jaggar were measuring a variety of volcanic phenomena that had been unknown just a few decades earlier.

Studying Kīlauea

Even better technology in the 1950s allowed volcano scientists to link their distant measuring stations to the central observatory site at Kīlauea's rim. With the more sensitive equipment they could not only track earth movements, which sometimes suggested underground movement of magma, but measure which areas were swelling and perhaps getting ready to erupt. Scientists followed the Kīlauea eruption of 1955 on the lower east rift zone and the Kīlauea Iki eruption of 1959, which sported huge lava fountains that people could drive to. The visual displays were dramatic but probably more interesting to the volcano scientists was using the new sophisticated equipment to study the swelling and subsiding of various parts of the summit as magma moved underground up and down, and back and forth.

In 1960, the volcano erupted next to the rural village of Kapoho. After its flows rumbled through the agricultural fields and burned home after home, all that remained was the old lighthouse at Cape Kumukahi. Following more than a dozen eruptions during the 1960s, Kīlauea entered a new kind of activity; the continuous eruption of Mauna Ulu lasted five years and shifted back and forth on the rift zone, forming shield and steep-sided cones. It sent lava flows down the side of the mountain and into the ocean, forming platforms of new solid land.

Studying Mauna Loa

During the 60s the Island of Hawai'i's other major attraction was quiet. Mauna Loa had erupted for 23 days in

Top: Scientists hold a morning meeting at a volcano overlook.

Center, top: The Mauna Ulu eruption of 1969 sent aerial fireworks into the sky not far from Kīlauea's summit. HAWAII VOLCANOES NATIONAL PARK

Center, bottom: Hawaiian Volcano Observatory founder Thomas Jaggar works in the Whitney Laboratory of Seismology in 1913 in what is now Hawai'i Volcanoes National Park.

Bottom: The lava pool at Halema'uma'u on September 19, 1974. GLEN KAYE

Lava flows near the coast with a distinct cone in the background. G. BRAD LEWIS

1950, then kept its peace for 25 years, ending with a one-day eruption at the summit crater of Moku'āweoweo in 1975 and again in 1984. Later on the same day it kicked off a new vent at an elevation of about 9,000 feet on its northeast rift zone, with high fountains in the chill mountain air. The eruption continued for three weeks, sending a long flow down the slope toward Hilo. The ribbon of black and orange lava extended for miles, but its leading edge was blocked just four miles short of Hilo. As a result, the flow broke out of the channel and sent a new flow parallel to the old one, reaching a little closer to Hilo. That channel became clogged again, and a third flow headed downslope. But by then, eruption was dropping off. On its 22nd day, it stopped.

Yet for months prior to this, Kīlauea had also been active. The Mauna Loa eruption answered one question volcano observers had debated for years: could two volcanoes erupt at once, or was there a single feeding route that pumped magma to one or the other, but not both? There had been overlapping eruptions of Kīlauea and Mauna Loa in 1919, although few people were aware of it. Chemical studies of the mineral and gas content of the lavas from the 1984 eruptions concluded that individual volcanoes have no connection near the surface, even though they ultimately all get their magma from deep within the same hot source in the mantle.

Above, top: Lava spatters into the air along the sea coast. Large amounts of molten rock can cause the water to steam and boil.
G. Brad Lewis

Above, bottom: Scientists study active lava flows at Kīlauea. Protective gear, including oxygen masks, is often mandatory.
G. Brad Lewis

Left: Gobs of molten rock are tossed skyward at Pu'u 'Ō'ō vent.
G. Brad Lewis

A sinewy river of lava runs from a vent on Kīlauea.

Kīlauea's Long One

FOR MORE THAN a century, from 1823 to 1924, Kīlauea maintained a nearly continuous lava lake. But until Mauna Ulu's eruption between 1969 and 1974, modern-era observers had not seen anything like an eruption that poured rock continuously down the slope of the volcano. For years on end, it covered existing countryside, raised the elevation of the slope and built up new land at the seashore. Mauna Ulu sent its lavas southward down the Kīlauea east rift zone over undeveloped land. The new rock covered parts of the Chain of Craters road and many archaeological sites on its way to the ocean, but no homes were threatened.

Then all the activity stopped and Mauna Ulu seemed to be an anomaly. That perception changed a decade later when in 1983 another east rift zone eruption of Kīlauea began that went on, and on. It was centered 12 miles out from the caldera, a long running eruption that set a new standard.

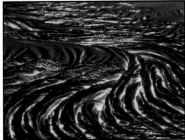

Tiltmeters and GPS

Volcano science was now more advanced than for any previous Kīlauea eruption. Sensors detected magma movement even before eruptions occurred. Tiltmeters measured the expansion and contraction of the summit and rifts of Kīlauea. As the eruption continued, new technologies were added to the geologists' toolboxes. Global positioning system satellite receivers, which became commonplace during the eruption, could measure with incredible accuracy the movement of the earth around the volcano. The result was that the eruption of Kīlauea that started in 1983 is probably the best-studied volcanic activity in the history of the planet.

The eruption began, as many do, with a subsurface rumble. The sophisticated seismic system, with its heart at the Hawaiian Volcano Observatory headquarters on the edge of Kīlauea's caldera, recorded swarms of earthquakes. These indicated that magma was moving deep underground and

Top: ***Pāhoehoe*** lava with its ridges cooling but its folds still incandescent. MICHAEL T. STEWART

Center: Orange molten rock bubbles from between sheets of hardened lava.

Bottom: Molten rock drips into the sea along the Kalapana coastline.

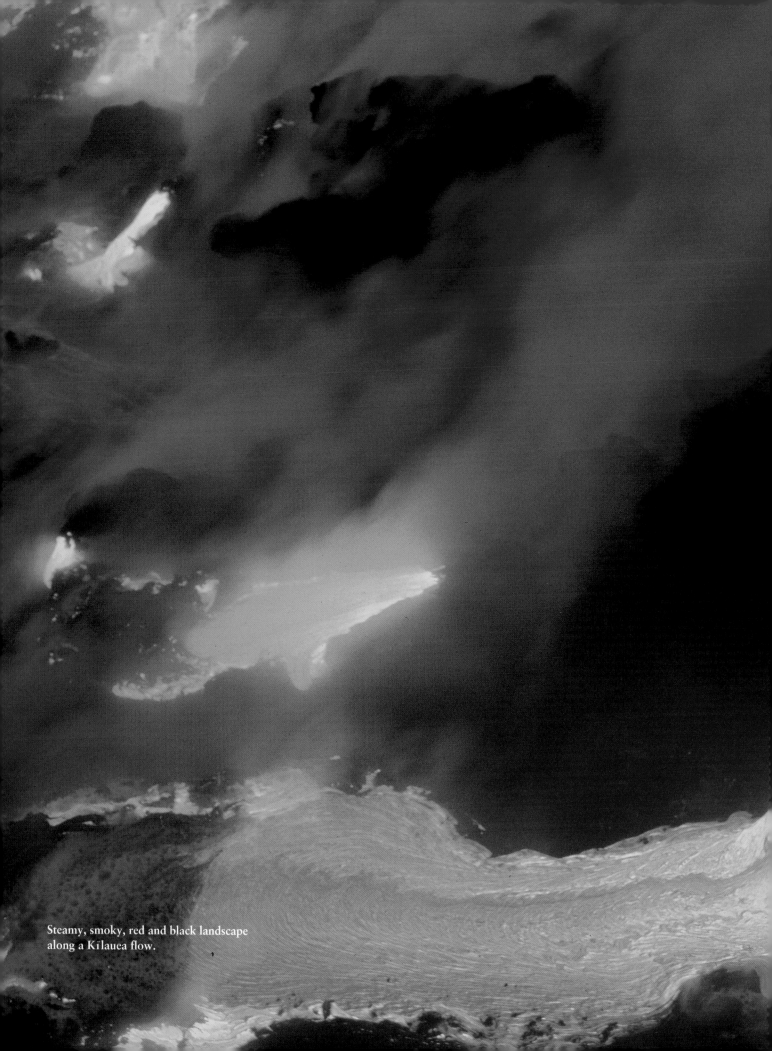

Steamy, smoky, red and black landscape
along a Kīlauea flow.

pushing into new channels creating a path for itself by ripping the rock apart. Just after midnight, the earth opened up at Nāpau Crater and fountains of orange lava danced into the night sky. The eruption spread up and down the east rift zone of Kīlauea, to Pu'u Kamoamoa, on to Pu'u Kahauale'a and back to Pu'u Kamoamoa. After ten hours the fountaining stopped briefly, but resumed with a 200-foot-high curtain of lava.

New Fountains

Scientists continued to measure the activity that occurred underground. On January 6, there were more fountains at Pu'u Kahauale'a and Pu'u Kamoamoa. The next day that activity went on and Pu'u Kalalua was added to it. Now, the eruption settled in, and lava began pooling and then spilling off the side of the mountain in a glowing flow.

The Kalapana coastline, downslope of Kīlauea's east rift zone, was not heavily populated. The Royal Gardens subdivision had roads but the developers had provided little else; no phones, water lines, electricity. Its network of paved roads headed steeply up the slope of the volcano. The 1, 500 lots were an acre each, but most lacked any kind of structure. About 50 had some variety of building on them, often very simple, rustic homes for a total of 150 people or so. The first flows headed directly toward the subdivision. More than half the residents were evacuated, but the lava stopped, and they moved back.

Volcanic Fumes

People living downwind in the South Kona area began feeling the discomfort living next door to an ongoing eruption. The volcanic fumes made their eyes water, and caused worsening health problems for those with respiratory ailments. Acid rain damaged vegetable and flower crops. Smoke from forest fires further degraded the air quality.

Flows continued to start and stop; some were the slower-moving *pāhoehoe*, appearing fluid and with a smooth surface that often had a ropelike texture; *'a'ā* flows tended to be thicker, with a leading edge of broken rock called clinker. On March 2, the first building burned as an *'a'ā* flow rolled in on Queen Avenue in Royal Gardens. A house-trailer burned right after it, the first home lost to lava flows since the Kapoho eruption in 1960.

Within four moths a quarter of the subdivision's empty lots were covered in black lava and eight buildings were reduced to ashes. By the end of the year, another eight had been destroyed.

Top: A fast moving *'a'ā* lava flow near the Pu'u 'Ō'ō vent on Kīlauea. G. Brad Lewis

Center, top: Kīlauea Volcano with a high fountain of lava shooting up close to the cone.

Center, bottom: Hot *pāhoehoe* lava, Puna. G. Brad Lewis

A volcanic fireworks spectacular. MICHAEL T. STEWART

The eruption now appeared to be centered and was creating a new cone. It was near the printed letter "o" on some maps that geologists used. After consulting with the Hawaiian community, the vent was named ʻŌʻō, and the cinder cone Puʻu ʻŌʻō, after a native bird of the forests, whose feathers were used for the capes of chiefs. Elders differed over the exact meaning; some preferred ʻōʻō, the name of the bird, while others argued for oʻo, meaning completed, or matured.

The eruption went on in episodes; dramatic activity with towering fountains, then a pause, then more eruption. Scientists gave each episode a new number. But since the magma appeared to be using the same underground channel to feed each eruption, and since the lava emissions occurred in the same limited complex of vents, it was all considered part of Kīlauea's long one.

Mauna Loa Joins In

In 1984, Mauna Loa erupted as well. The staff at the Hawaiian Volcano Observatory was under tremendous strain to keep track of two eruptions at once. As Mauna Loa sent a long flow northeast toward Hilo, Kīlauea ran an entirely new flow southward down the east rift zone to Royal Gardens. Civil Defense officials expanded their areas of evacuation, including a number of homes in the older neighboring community of Kalapana. By mid-April, both Kīlauea and Mauna Loa had subsided without destroying any homes. But in the third week of the month, Kīlauea made its first entry into an inhabited area outside Royal Gardens.

The most southerly development of the lower Puna coastline was the hillside subdivision of Royal Gardens. Immediately to the northeast, along the coast road, there was the old, predominately Hawaiian rural community of Kapaʻahu. Farther along were the clustered homes of Kalapana, which had both old lots and Kalapana Gardens, a subdivision full of mostly new residents. Beyond that were a few structures around Kaimū black sand beach. The gathering place for residents and the eruption watchers in the region was Kalapana Store and Drive-In, next to the Mauna Kea Congregational Church, and across the street from the famed Painted Church of Kalapana. Another gathering place was the pavilion and picnic tables of Harry K. Brown Park. All of these areas would suffer a similar fate.

Sites Lost

There were many historic sites in the region, starting with the important Wahaʻula Heiau complex,

Top: Continuous eruption builds up promontories on the landscape as the lava flows pile up, one on top of the other.

Center: Flows establish rivers through low areas. As these fill, the molten rock finds new routes, filling one depression after another.

Bottom: Lava flows readily through vegetated areas, as here in Kalapana Gardens. Sometimes lava filled the area beneath homes built on poles, producing a steady, fierce heat that made the building burst into flame only after the lava front had moved on.

Steam pours off the cliffs overlooking Kīlauea lava lake.

dated at 1275 A.D. In addition the area had Hawaiian village remains, other *heiau* or temples, canoe landing sites, trails, coastal habitation and refuge caves, the famed clear waters of Queen's Bath and much more. It was difficult to walk far without coming across remains of early habitation.

The regular eruptions at Puʻu ʻŌʻō built up a cone several hundred feet high over lava flows that had raised the level of the surrounding land. By mid-1986, Puʻu ʻŌʻō was 800 feet higher than the land had been before the eruption. Geologists at the Hawaiian Volcano Observatory recorded 47 different episodes that started in 1983, and in the 3-1/2 years of activity, an estimated 26 million cubic meters of lava had been erupted onto the slopes of an east rift zone.

But now something changed. On July 18, 1986, the eruption abandoned Puʻu ʻŌʻō and moved to a series of new cracks, creating a mile-long curtain of molten rock. Activity settled in at a location that came to be known as Kupaianaha, and stayed there for the next five and a half years. This site was about two miles farther out the rift zone than Puʻu ʻŌʻō, and put lava more directly uphill from inhabited areas. The Kūpaianaha vent sent flow after flow down the mountain. By late November, hot lava was back threatening a coastal village.

Lava Moves

Lava flowing on the surface normally moves fairly slowly unless it is on a steep slope or in a lava channel. But a long-lasting flow often creates a lava tube system, which changes the dynamics, especially for people with properties at the far lower end. As a flow moves, its sides and top cool and begin to crust over, while lava continues to flow inside the hardened crust, creating a long tube, through which the hot molten rock moves without the cooling effects of winds and rain. Lava in these tube systems can be sampled through skylights, which are holes in the tops of the new tubes. Skylights often are formed when pieces of the tube roof collapse. Thus, tubes make it possible for still-fluid, fast-moving, hot lava to be delivered right down to the coast, retaining its destructive capabilities.

In late 1986 lava suddenly poured into the town of Kapaʻahu, destroying eight homes, utility lines and roads. This was a severe blow to the community. While the Royal Gardens subdivision had been mainly occupied by new residents without extensive roots in the region, the people of Kapaʻahu had lived there for generations, raising children and grandchildren in the same wood-frame houses, their favorite plants carefully tended in their yards. The lava

Top: The flows from Puʻu ʻŌʻō spared the Wahaʻula Heiau complex in the early years, but eventually built up the land around the sacred site, and flowed into the interior areas until very little of the original structures remained uncovered.

Center: Lava flows underground through huge tubes. Visitors to Nāhuku (Thurston Lava Tube) in Hawaiʻi Volcanoes National Park can follow the trail of an ancient flow.

Bottom: A Kīlauea Volcano view.

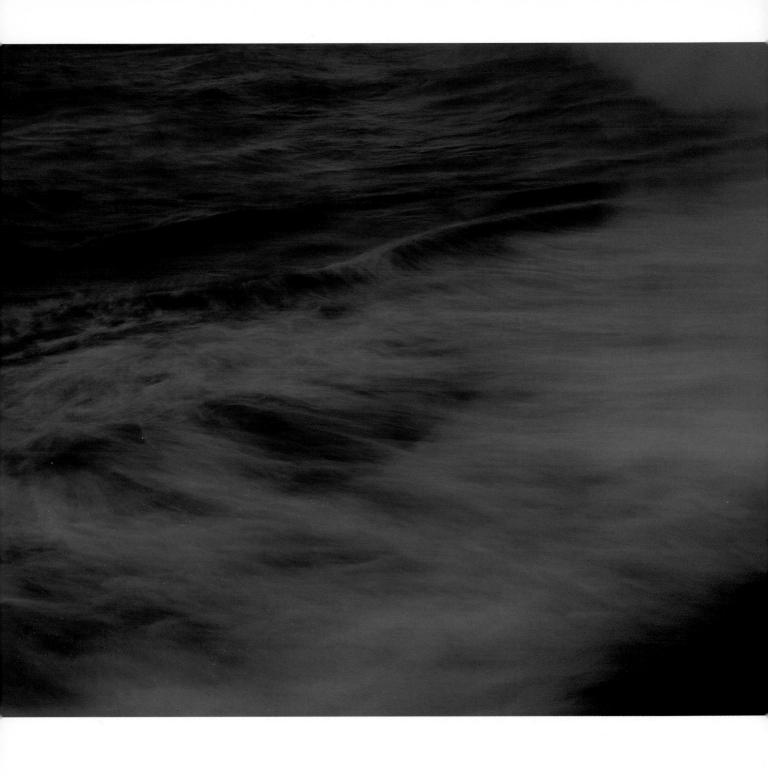

flowed through their properties, reached the barrier of the
raised Kalapana Highway, and then simply waited while
more and more lava backed up behind the highway. Finally,
the crusted lava lake was high enough and smoking rock
slipped across the tarmac. That flow separated the eastern
and western Kalapana coastline. Children in Royal
Gardens' remaining homes had to commute 50 miles
through Volcano and Kea'au to get to school in Pāhoa.
Their neighbors, on the other side of the flow, had just a
10-mile ride. The lava went on, steaming and hissing. On
the one hand, the flow poured rock continually into the

Above: At the ocean's edge, the lava
flow is repeatedly cooled by contrast
with water, then breaks through and
pushes forward as the waves retreat.

Spectators view an eruption at Hawai'i Volcanoes National Park. Such a close encounter with raw lava is not always possible, due to the presence of toxic gases and the sheer unpredictability of volcanoes. The extreme heat generated by a field of molten rock can also limit the approach of anyone not wearing thick, protective gear. G. BRAD LEWIS

sea, creating 20 acres of new land within a few weeks. But on the other hand, it followed a path of destruction, inching eastward toward Kalapana. On December 17, the first home was burned, and three days later, 17 more were gone. Many residents were evacuated to a Red Cross shelter at Pāhoa, or camped nearer home in Harry K. Brown Park. Those who still had homes were able to spend Christmas there.

Kalapana tried to get back to a normal life. The county ran bulldozers over the still-warm rocks to allow cars to drive along the original rock to the Kalapana Highway, but by the end of March 1987, lava once again crossed the road. Molten rock poured into the historic natural bathing pool Punaluʻu, known as Queen's Bath, which hissed and boiled as the lava crept through. The only remaining Royal Gardens access, a footpath, was covered, and then the flows moved westward toward National Park Service buildings. In June and July 1989, despite efforts to divert the flows by spraying them with water from tanker trucks, the park's complex was lost. Thick sheets of lava seeped under the buildings, heating them until they burst into flame. Afterwards, only iron roofing and metal girders lay on the surface of the flow.

Pali Diversion

In 1990, the activity moved back to the east. There a geological feature helped ensure the final destruction of Kalapana. The Hakuma Pali, a cliff standing between the coast and the village prevented flows from reaching the sea. Instead, they turned left and poured through Kalapana Gardens and old Kalapana.

It was the end of the community. To those directly affected, the volcano seemed to be in a single-minded mopping-up mode. Lava oozed this way and that, ultimately engulfing everything. Every single home in Kalapana village was destroyed. Some thought Pele would save the churches. But the Congregational church burned. In a heroic effort, residents and friends hoisted up the Painted Church, which was across the road and closer to the beach, and carried it out of harm's way.

Yet the sense of loss went far beyond just the structures. The peaceful character of the land was altered. As earlier flows had consumed the Queen's Bath and other prehistoric sites, this series of flows covered Kaimū Bay. Hissing lava flowed into Kalapana surfing areas.

The eruption was nearly continuous from 1986 to 1992, and it created a broad shield, Kūpaianalua a new feature on the east rift zone. It produced an estimated 41

Top: A Kalapana home set afire by the relentless flow that could not be diverted.

Center: The scenic Kaimū black sand beach was covered by flows after most of the neighboring Kalapana Village had already been destroyed.

Bottom: Punaluʻu (Queen's Bath) was a cool natural pool, with worn stones that recalled centuries of use as a recreational site for early Hawaiian visitors and recent arrivals. It was covered by the Kīlauea flows.

Continued fountaining builds the cones that dot the volcanic

million cubic meters of lava. The communities of Royal Gardens, Kapaʻahu and Kalapana were no more. By now, 181 houses had been wiped out, along with the Wahaʻula visitor center and innumerable archaeological sites. With the destruction of the buildings, and the departure of the residents, much of the media and public interest in the eruption waned. The eruption was once more less of a people story and more of a geological curiosity. But the volcano kept on.

Vast Destruction

On February 7, 1992, the eruption moved back uprift to Puʻu ʻŌʻō in what scientists calculated as the long-running eruption's 50th episode. For curious non-scientists, it was too difficult and dangerous to hike out to the vent, where gases were toxic and the lava unstable. But a comparatively safe visit could be made to the edge of activity at the shoreline. Visitors frequently took extreme risks and walked over cooling flows to get near where lava was pouring into the sea. The coastal lava benches regularly collapsed, and officials were kept busy trying to control thrill-seekers who did not understand the danger. It was a year-round show that attracted thousands, despite acrid clouds of steam containing hydrochloric acid and sulfur dioxide. At the shoreline, the area covered by lava was almost six miles wide.

Campers Surprised

Local attention continued to be focused on the shoreline through the early and middle 1990s, then a change in upslope activity reoriented public attention. On January 30, 1997, two campers at Nāpau Crater were awakened by shuddering ground and an unearthly roar. Kīlauea had changed sites again. The terrified campers scrambled to safety as the volcano broke through again where the eruption had started back in 1983.

There were several episodes of fountaining, but then Kīlauea grew quiet. Three weeks later, some observers began predicting that the flurry of activity had been a last gasp; the eruption could be over. Yet with episode 55, Puʻu ʻŌʻō kicked back into gear. At first just some rising and falling of lava deep in the crater itself and the lava lake next to it, but soon the flow of magma to the Puʻu ʻŌʻō site was re-established, and the eruption was back in familiar territory. No one knew how long it would last.

The wide river of lava formed by the 1984 eruption of
Mauna Loa. The eruption coincided with the long-running
Kīlauea eruption. Scott Lopez, Hawaii Volcanoes National Park

Mauna Loa

MASSIVE, RISING NEARLY three miles above sea level, and extending another three miles down to the sea floor, Mauna Loa is the biggest volcano on the planet in terms of volume. But its time is passing. Geologists figure the center of Mauna Loa has drifted past the Hawaiian hot spot, though it is still being fed magma. Kīlauea, which may be nearly right over the hot spot, is believed to be fed directly, while Loʻihi is apparently at the leading edge of the hot spot. Both Kīlauea and Lōʻihi have formed on the flanks of Mauna Loa, yet are considered to be distinct volcanoes.

Mauna Loa itself has erupted 23 times in the past century. Two of these eruptions, in 1940 and 1949, lasted more than 100 days. One in 1903 lasted 60 days, and none of the rest went on for more than 50. Most commonly, the duration was for a week or two. The volcano sent out very fluid lavas, which moved quickly down the slopes. Five flows have reached the ocean since 1868.

Archibald Menzies

The first European to climb Mauna Loa was Archibald Menzies, a famed botanist who visited with Captain George Vancouver in 1793 and 1794. Menzies arranged with the new king, Kamehameha, for a trek up the mountain. It is an indication of how difficult the travel was that he only made it to the summit on his third attempt. In these days of paved roads and high-powered vehicles, it is almost impossible to understand the difficulties faced by early travelers.

The volcanic landscape and the distances on the Island of Hawaiʻi argued for an initial approach by ocean. Menzies left his ship on a double canoe with 20 paddlers. Their first night was spent at Hōnaunau, just a short distance down the coast. The next day's run was a long one, to Honomalino, a small sandy bay where they loaded up on coconuts and spent the night. The sea was rough when they arrived at Manukā for the third night, and the black cliffs and boulders of the coast appeared dangerous.

Top: Mauna Loa stands 13,677 feet above sea level, a typical Hawaiian shield volcano.

Center: Eruptions on Mauna Loa are generally not as long as those of Kīlauea, but produce vast amounts of lava in short periods of time.

Bottom: Mauna Loa's summit features the vast caldera of Mokuʻāweoweo. G. BRAD LEWIS

A Lunar Landscape

The sheer size and breadth of Mauna Loa amazed the first foreigners to see its summit. Today the sight is no less impressive. This largely barren, lunar landscape does not seem to fit in the usual picture of a Hawai'i consisting of lush plants, brilliant flowers and lovely beaches. Mauna Loa may have erupted in 1780, shortly after Captain Cook's final visit, but the mountain appears to have remained quiet from then into the next century.

Aerial view of the Mauna Loa summit. The small white areas are patches of snow.
G. Brad Lewis

Menzies could not see how they were going to land, but the double canoe's crew set up just offshore and waited for the right wave.

Perilous Landing

The botanist's account continues in a tone of amazement: "With this surge they dashed in, landed up on a rock from which we scrambled up the precipice and in an instant about 50 or 60 of the natives at the word of command shouldered the canoe with everything in her, and clambering up the rugged steep, lodged her safety in a large canoe house upon the brink of the precipice, to our utmost astonishment." They were able to watch as a second canoe was successfully brought ashore the same way.

The dexterity of the Hawaiians in the ocean, even where it crashed onto the rocks, was a matter of fascination to these Europeans. Menzies found it amazing that the native residents were able to convert the rugged landscape into a place for sport. He wrote of daring female cliff divers: "A number of young women...stripped themselves quite naked upon the summit of a pending cliff, and taking a short run vaulted one after another from the brink of it headlong into the sea regardless of the foamed and agitated appearance of that element, and as it were setting its wildest commotions at defiance, for at this time the surf ran very high and dashed with furious force against the cliff, yet they dexteriously disentangled themselves and clambering up the rock again, repeated their leaps several times with seeming satisfaction till they were quite fatigued. The cliff was at least thirty feet height and so very rugged with packed rocks which were now and then deluged with a boisterous surf, that to look down the precipice was enough to intimidate any one not accustomed to such extraordinary feats of activity."

Plantation Hike

The expedition then went on by foot up the southeastern side of the island. They passed through fields of grass, and plantations of bananas, *kalo* and sweet potatoes. Menzies the botanist made note that in this dry countryside, the natives mulched their cultivated fields with grass "to preserve them from the powerful heat of the sun."

They passed through Punalu'u and reached Kapāpala, where they began a direct route to the summit. Although the eruption records don't refer to a Kīlauea eruption in 1794, Menzies felt there must have been one

Top: A Mauna Loa sunrise.
G. BRAD LEWIS

Center: The vast Moku'āweoweo Caldera on Mauna Loa spreads out below a rim of steep cliffs. Mauna Kea is in the background.
G. BRAD LEWIS

Bottom: A hiker descending from the summit of Mauna Loa finds the way carpeted with stretches of unmelted snow.
G. BRAD LEWIS

Following page: Lua Poholo crater, in Moku'āweoweo caldera, apparently formed in 1880.
G. BRAD LEWIS

Distant volcanoes and nearby forests form a typical Island of Hawaiʻi setting, yet one not often associated with so-called "tropical" Hawaiʻi. G. BRAD LEWIS

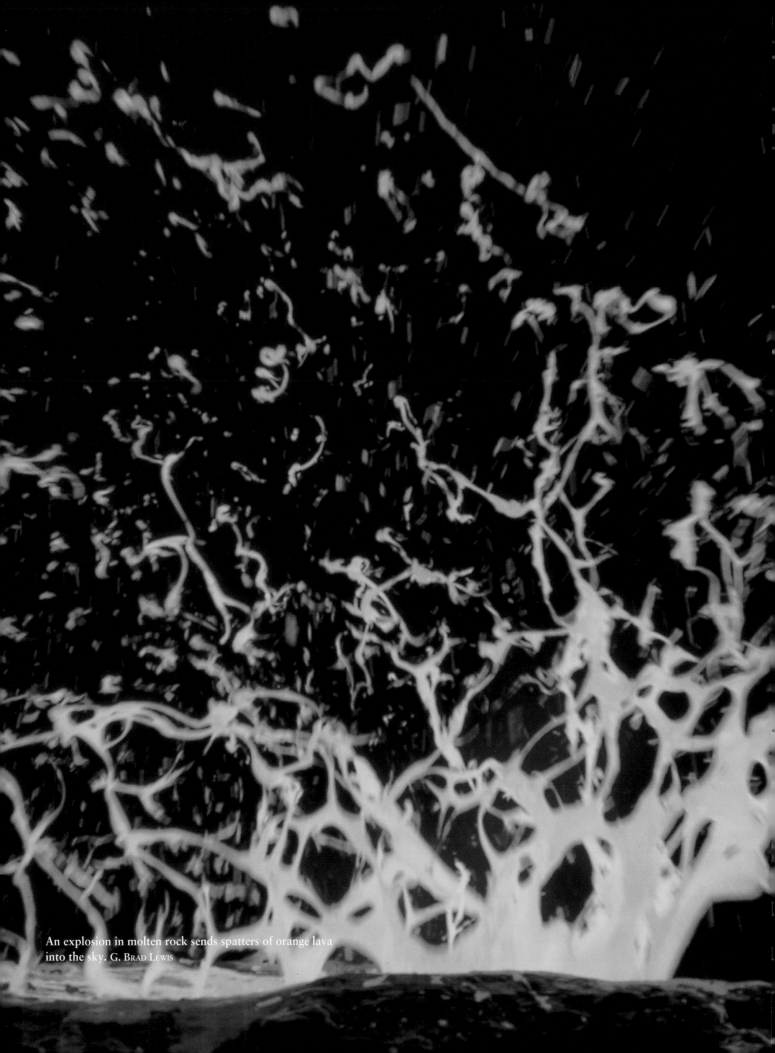

An explosion in molten rock sends spatters of orange lava into the sky. G. Brad Lewis

because of the smoke and ash blowing down the southeast flank. He complained that the air was "very thick" and "very tormenting to our eyes." They headed uphill on February 13 from an elevation of 1,800 feet. Menzies used a barometer, using the declining atmospheric pressure that occurs with rising altitude to calculate his elevation above sea level. By the end of the day they had reached 3,510 feet. The next afternoon, they found frost on the ground. On February 15, they passed the tree line at 10,543 feet, and camped at 11,515 feet. The weather was below freezing, and since they were too high to find wood for a fire, they burned their walking sticks to cook hot chocolate, which they drank with a little rum.

Rum and Coconuts

On the morning of the 16th, 10 days into the expedition, their only remaining provisions were a few coconuts, a little chocolate and part of a bottle of rum. Menzies reached the edge of Mauna Loa's summit caldera, Mokuʻāweoweo, just before noon. He calculated its elevation at 13,635 feet, which is just 40 feet short of modern figures. Decades later, observers still made errors of thousands of feet guessing its height. The summit caldera had cliffs 400 yards high, Menzies figured, and was a mile across. The bottom of the caldera was flat, with a rough texture and hot steam rising from two or three places at its edge.

The next well-documented climb up Mauna Loa was by another Scottish botanist, David Douglas, who later died in Hawaiʻi under mysterious circumstances. He also went up on the route from Kapāpala in January 1834, and had to trudge through deep snow to reach the edge of Mokuʻāweoweo.

Hawaiian Guides

While these men may have led the first expeditions that included Europeans, it seems clear that they walked in Polynesian footsteps. After all, both were shown the proper route by Hawaiians. It is near the present ʻAinapo trail, which even today is one of the three main routes to the summit. In 1794 ʻAinapo provided the shortest distance to the top from a place where provisions could be acquired at that time.

The first serious surveying trip apparently went up near the present-day Mauna Loa Trail. This ascends from Kīlauea along the northeast rift and reaches Mokuʻāweoweo from the east or northeast, while Menzies and Douglas approached from the southeast. The United States Exploring

Top: Old lava flows in the foreground have weathered to a brownish tint, while the newer lavas below in the caldera remain dark gray. G. Brad Lewis

Center: Several Hawaiian volcanoes are high enough to be regularly seen above the clouds. This photo is taken from Mauna Loa looking toward Mauna Kea. G. Brad Lewis

Bottom: Hikers cross the rugged, ancient lava flows of Mauna Loa. G. Brad Lewis

Lava tube on Mauna Loa volcano.
G. Brad Lewis

Expedition, under the command of Lt. Charles Wilkes of the USS *Vincennes*, headed up in December 1840. The men built a small compound on the mountain, with high walls to break the force of the wind during their stay. Wilkes spent nearly a month there. His choice of route provides one proof that the Hawaiians knew the way up the mountain: they told Wilkes that he had taken the wrong way, and indeed he had difficulties that could have been avoided. Wilkes nevertheless produced the first surveyed chart of the top of the world's biggest mountain in terms of height and mass from bottom to top.

Since that time, Mauna Loa has been thoroughly studied. Instruments track its every shudder and quake. But hiking the mountain is still an extreme challenge, a four or five-day affair, even starting at 6,662 feet at the end of Mauna Loa Strip Road, and even with the help of two cabins, one 7 miles up the trail, and the other 11 miles farther on, near the summit. Travelers still come from all over the world to make the climb.

Above, top: **Mauna Kea in the distance and Mauna Loa in the foreground often rise like twin islands in the sky, both projecting through the clouds.**

Above, middle: **The cabin at the summit of Mauna Loa, where visitors who have made the arduous hike to the top can seek overnight shelter.** G. BRAD LEWIS

Above, bottom: **Scientists probe the Earth's atmosphere from the Mauna Loa Observatory, high on the slopes of the volcano.** G. BRAD LEWIS

A deep submersible craft is lowered into the ocean off the
Island of Hawaiʻi for reconnaissance work on the growing
undersea island of Lōʻihi. FRED DUENNEBIER

Lōʻihi

Hawaiʻi's YOUNGEST VOLCANO, 20 miles off the southeast coast of Hawaiʻi, has its summit still 3,100 feet below the surface of the ocean. Like Kīlauea, Lōʻihi is growing on the (undersea) slope of Mauna Loa, the largest active volcano in the world. Studies of the earthquakes under Lōʻihi show that the shallower events are near the present location of the volcanic seamount, but down deep they converge with the quakes under Kīlauea. Scientists feel this shows that Kīlauea and Lōʻihi are tapping the same magma source, the Hawaiian Hot Spot, as does Mauna Loa. However, studies of the actual rock erupted by the three volcanoes show that it is chemically different. It's not clear why this is the case.

For a long time, Lōʻihi lay undiscovered, and even after scientists became aware of it, they weren't sure it was an active volcano. That changed with improved earthquake monitoring techniques. In 1970, equipment on the Island of Hawaiʻi registered a swarm of earthquakes and scientists were able to calculate their location: Lōʻihi. The volcano has been fairly quiet in recent years, but in July 1996 Lōʻihi broke into the most active swarm of quakes ever measured on any Hawaiian volcano: more than 4,000 within a month.

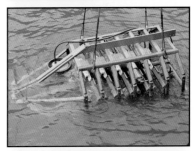

Deep Submersible

By this time, scientists had the technology to go down and see what was going on. Using a deep submersible vehicle, a specialized submarine, they found the quake of 1996 had left a vast caldera. Not surprisingly, it was shaped much like the one atop Kīlauea. Other features of the undersea mountaintop had been obliterated. Scientists believed the magma chamber under the summit suddenly filled underground cracks rather than erupting onto the surface. The earthquakes resulted from shuddering associated with the cracking of rock as magma forced its way up through the ocean floor. The scientists who arrived within days of the activity also found it was difficult to see

Top: Researchers check the readings on their instruments as they study Lōʻihi, monitoring all subterranean quakes. Fred Duennebier

Center: Scientific equipment for studying an undersea volcano is lowered by cables from the main research ship. Fred Duennebier

Bottom: Instruments measuring the activity of the undersea volcano Lōʻihi rest on the sea floor. Fred Duennebier

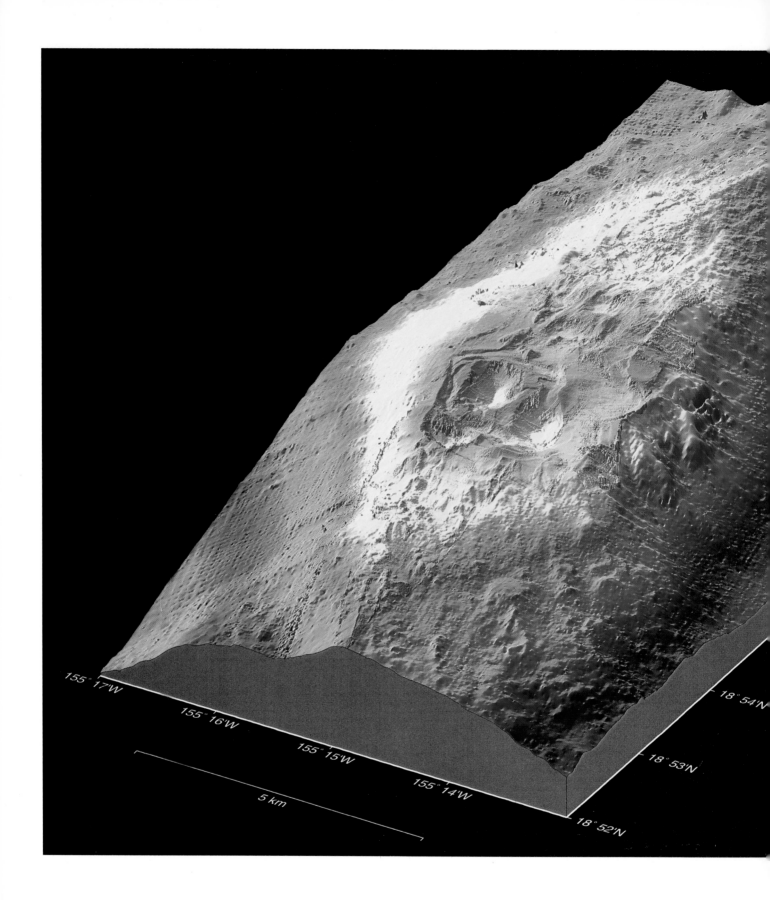

155° 17'W

155° 16'W

155° 15'W

155° 14'W

18° 54'N

18° 53'N

18° 52'N

5 km

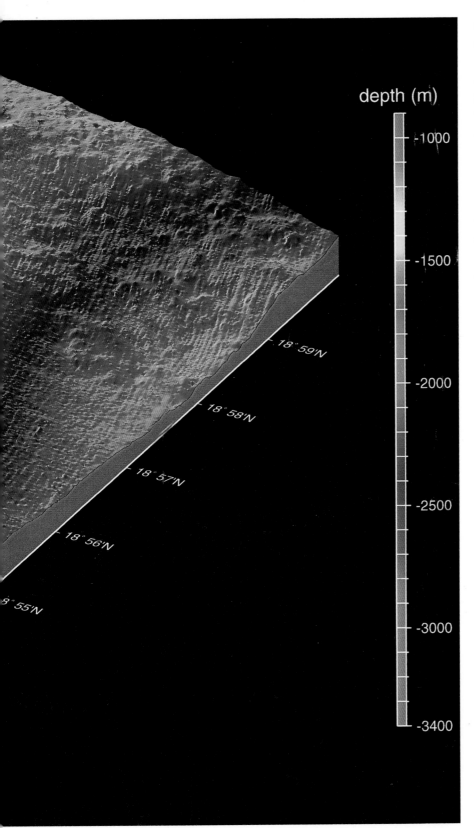

depth (m)

-1000

-1500

-2000

-2500

-3000

-3400

18° 59'N

18° 58'N

18° 57'N

18° 56'N

8° 55'N

anything because Lōʻihi was shrouded in clouds and sediment.

All Hawaiian volcanoes begin as submarine volcanoes, and rise as much as three miles before they break the surface of the ocean. Lōʻihi actually started in somewhat shallower waters, since it already stands on the submerged slope of another volcano. The early eruptions of Hawaiian volcanoes generally can't be detected by the eye at the surface. The pressure of the deep ocean water prevents explosive events, but the volcanoes still erupt, and lava is released. One feature of these eruptions is pillow lava, large mushroom or pillow-shaped extrusions with comparatively smooth surfaces. This undersea rock, which hardens very fast in the cool ocean water, tends to be brittle and glass-like. Submerged volcanoes are torn and shaken by earthquakes just like surface volcanoes, and their appearance can be changed dramatically.

Lōʻihi is a very steep volcano, much-fractured and thus porous. Sea water is thought to flow readily among its surface rocks. Some geologists also believe that a strong future eruption could produce a huge landslide, large enough to create a catastrophic tsunami. However, like so much speculation about volcanoes, this is an educated guess, a theory that might or might not be valid.

Left: A scan of the ocean floor off Hawaiʻi island reveals the growing volcano, Lōʻihi. It is already a large mountain, but it remains thousands of feet below the ocean's surface.

At Keauhou Landing in Ka'u, earth movement and new lava flows have produced distinct volcanic plateaus.

Slides

As GEOLOGICAL FEATURES, volcanoes are often steep but are not a solid mass. Their rock is extensively fractured, and different portions are subjected to a range of forces, such as gravity or the expansion and contraction of active volcanoes. Sometimes those forces cause sudden movements in the form of deep unfelt earthquakes, measurable only with sensitive equipment. More powerful movements can produce massive changes on land and in the surrounding sea. Just as a motion in a bathtub causes ripples in the water, a movement of land along the coast can cause tsunami, ocean waves that result in extreme damage to shoreline areas many miles away.

You can do a simple experiment to show how many earthquakes occur. Wet your hands, then dry them and press the palms together. Now begin forcing them in different directions. Push the right hand toward the fingers and the left hand toward the wrist. If the hands are dry, but not too dry, friction holds them in place until the pressure grows sufficiently to overcome it. Eventually, your hands slip, then stop, with the fingers of the right hand now overlapping those on the left. The same principles apply for huge land masses.

Quake Falls

In an earthquake two sections of land are forced in different directions by pressures deep in the Earth. Generally at established fault lines, they slip, and the sudden release of energy produces vibrations that travel through the rock, creating an earthquake.

Sometimes such an earth movement can cause dramatic settling and changes in the landscape. A powerful earthquake in 1975 caused a section of volcanic coastline to suddenly subside; at Halapē, where the resulting tsunami killed two people, the subsidence left a grove of coconut trees standing in several feet of sea water. Hawaiian traditions record other severe earthquakes that also caused land changes.

Top: Land and sea meet in a confusion of white surf along the Puna coast.

Center: Small offshore islands can be the result of wind and sea erosional forces that cut away weaker rocks, or could be remnants of giant landslides that tear off chunks of the neighboring island mass.

Bottom: Rugged cliffs, as here on the North Kohala coastline, show evidence of recent landslides, which shear away sections of rock that pile along the cliff bottoms.

Rugged, rocky and remote, the roadless stretch of north Moloka'i coastline is often shaded by clouds.

But perhaps the most impressive quake-related land movement is a massive event in which a whole section of the island disappears in a giant undersea landslide. Underwater mapping techniques now suggest that there have been many such slides around most of the large islands. Mapping of the sea floor has located large debris fields, many of them at the bottom of sea cliffs.

Such events must be so huge, and associated with such forceful *tsunami,* that it's a good thing no human has seen one. Certain geologists believe evidence of coral and other debris at 900 feet in elevation on the Island of Lāna'i are the result of a tsunami associated with a massive Hawai'i marine avalanche.

Moloka'i's Cliffs

Some of the highest sea cliffs in Hawai'i are on the north coast of east Moloka'i. Ocean floor mapping shows basalt boulders and other debris extending out 100 miles north of those cliffs.

There is a similar phenomenon on O'ahu's north coast, off the steep cliffs that stand mauka of Kane'ohe and the region on both sides of it. There are slide areas off Kaua'i and Ni'ihau as well. In all, scientists have located 15 big slide areas around Hawai'i's islands. They consider them to be massive, even on a planetary scale.

The big slides provide students of Hawai'i volcanoes with a remarkable tool. By breaking away sections of land that have been laid down roughly horizontally, they provide a cutaway view of the geological history of the Islands in the form of layer upon layer of old lava flows.

One could reasonably speculate that enormous landslides—large enough to create tsunami—are not a daily threat, particularly on the older islands with dead or dormant volcanoes. Presumably these volcanic slides where huge cliffs broke off into the ocean occurred in the distant past, before Hawai'i was populated. But thorough study and dating of these fields of slide debris still has to be done. And who can say what a volcano has in store? After all, Lō'ihi is a very young island and might have a sudden growth spurt that could surprise us all.

Top: The steep cliffs of the north shore of Moloka'i, viewed from far to the north.

Center: These agricultural uplands drop precipitously to the sea, showing the typical pattern of slide erosion.

Bottom: Sea stacks, prominent ridgelines, and steep-sided valleys mark Moloka'i's northern coast. Such huge chunks of rock may have been hurled into the ocean by an ancient earthquake.

Moloka'i's north shore has few
protected inlets, and is generally
only accessible by boat, and only in
the summer, since powerful surf in
winter prevents coastal travel. This
landscape shows dramatic evidence
of geological upheaval in the distant

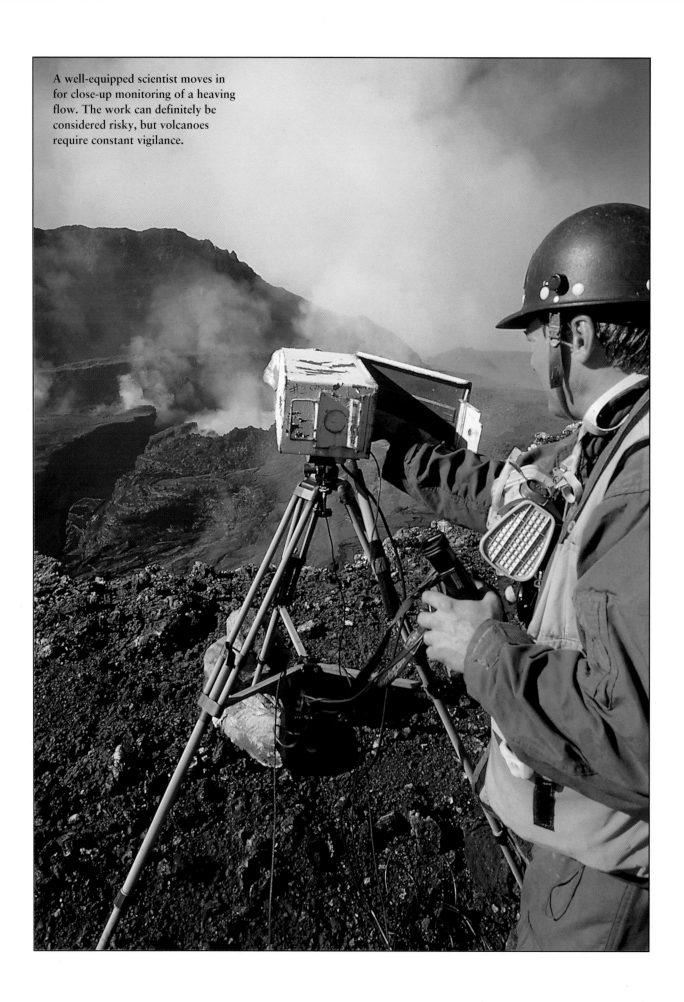

A well-equipped scientist moves in for close-up monitoring of a heaving flow. The work can definitely be considered risky, but volcanoes require constant vigilance.

Glossary

'a'ā — an often slow-moving type of Hawaiian lava that has a jagged surface after cooling; a stage of cooled lava which resembles gravelly cinders.

atoll — a mountainous volcano that has eroded over millions of years into a flat little island shaped like a ring or crescent, and covered in coral or surrounded by a coral reef.

basalt — volcanic rock that heats to the melting point, appears as lava and turns dark brown or black when it cools and hardens.

coral reefs — the skeletons of millions of tiny marine animals which settle on the underwater slopes of a new volcano. Large reefs typically grow around all Pacific volcanoes as a stage of development lasting many millennia.

eruption — a sudden outburst of lava, rock and gases caused by an extreme build-up of pressure under the Earth's crust.

guyot — an atoll that has sunk below the surface of the water; a final stage in the erosion of a volcanic peak.

hot spot — a specific location where magma breaks through the Earth's crust to create a volcano, which over a long period of time may become part of a series of volcanoes.

lava — molten rock which has come up from the Earth's mantle in liquid form, and spatters, flows or fountains along the surface until it cools and hardens.

magma — melted rock found beneath the Earth's crust, beginning at the upper mantle which can start anywhere from 5-30 miles underground.

pāhoehoe — the other main type of Hawaiian lava, fast-moving, and resembling thick, black concrete oozing from a pump, and glowing with red and orange fire.

plate tectonics — theories developed in the 1960s which base all volcanic activity on the location and movement of massive sections of the planet defined as "plates." The Hawaiian Islands are situated on the Pacific Plate.

seamount — a mountain whose peak is below the surface of the ocean, and which may have once been an island but has eroded.

volcanic phases — 1) initial eruption, 2) shield building, 3) dormancy, erosion and subsidence. The phase of rejuvenation may occur between 2 and 3, in which case dormancy is considerably delayed.

tiltmeters — scientific instruments for measuring the expansion and contraction of various portions of a live volcano.

Bibliography

Beckwith, Martha, 1972 (translation). "The Kumulipo: A Hawaiian Creation Chant." University of Hawaii Press, Honolulu. (First published by University of Chicago Press, Chicago, 1951.)

Beckwith, Martha, 1970. "Hawaiian Mythology." University of Hawaii Press, Honolulu. (First published by Yale University Press, New Haven, 1940.)

Bingham, Hiram; 1848. "A Residence of Twenty-One Years in the Sandwich Islands." Second edition. Hartford: Hezekiah Huntington: New York: Sherman Converse. (First published 1947.)

Bird, Isabella L., 1894. "Six Months in the Sandwich Islands." G.P. Putnam's Sons, New York. (First published 1875, London.)

Brassey, Mrs. Annie., 1881. "A Voyage in the 'Sunbeam.'" Belford, Clarke & Co., Chicago.

Carlquist, Sherwin, 1980. "Hawaii: A Natural History." Pacific Tropical Botanical Garden, Lawai, Kauai.

Day, A. Grove, editor, 1975. "Mark Twain's Letters from Hawaii." University Press of Hawaii, Honolulu. (Reprint of edition by Appleton-Century, New York.)

Elbert, Samuel H., editor, 1959. "Selections from Fornander's 'Hawaiian Antiquities and Folk-Lore.'" University of Hawaii Press, Honolulu.

Geography, Department of, University of Hawaii, 1973. "Atlas of Hawaii." University Press of Hawaii, Honolulu.

I'i, John Papa, 1959. "Fragments of Hawaiian History." Translated by Mary Kawena Pukui. Bishop Museum Press, Honolulu. (First published in Hawaiian in the newspaper *Kuokoa,* 1866 to 1870.)

Kay, E. Alison, editor, 1994. "A Natural History of the Hawaiian Islands, Selected Readings II." University of Hawaii Press, Honolulu.

Kaye, Glen, 1976. "Hawaii Volcanoes: The Story Behind the Scenery." KC Publications, Las Vegas.

Krauss, Bob, 1992. "Birth by Fire: A Guide to Hawaii's Volcanoes." Island Heritage Publishing, Aiea.

Kuykendall, Ralph S., 1938. "A History of Hawaii. " The Macmillan Company, New York.

Malo, David, 1971. "Hawaiian Antiquities (Moolelo Hawaii)." Bishop Museum Press, Honolulu. (Translated from Hawaiian by Dr. Nathaniel B. Emerson, 1898.)

Pukui, Mary K., Samuel H. Elbert and Esther T. Mookini, 1974. "Place Names of Hawaii." University Press of Hawaii, Honolulu. (First published 1966.)

TenBruggencate, Jan, Robert Hollis and Michael deGruy, 1990. "Hawaii's Kilauea Volcano: The Flow to the Sea." C.F. Boone Publishing Co., Sun City West, Arizona. (First published 1987.)

Wagner, Warren L. and V.A. Funk, editors, 1995. "Hawaiian Biogeography: Evolution on a Hot Spot Archipelago." Smithsonion Institution Press, Washington and London.

Westervelt, William D., 1977. "Hawaiian Historical Legends." Charles E. Tuttle Co., Rutland, Vermont, and Tokyo. (Reprint of 1923 edition, Fleming H. Revell Co., New York.)

Westervelt, William D., 1973. "Hawaiian Legends of Volcanoes." Charles E. Tuttle Co., Rutland, Vermont and Tokyo. (Reprint of 1916 editions in U.S and Britain.)

Wright, Thomas L., Taeko Jane Takahashi and J.D. Griggs, 1992. "Hawai'i Volcano Watch; A Pictorial History, 1779-1991." University of Hawaii Press, Honolulu.

Index